Of poets, gods, ghosts, irritants and storytellers: *Diagramatologically unleashed*

Tendai Rinos Mwanaka

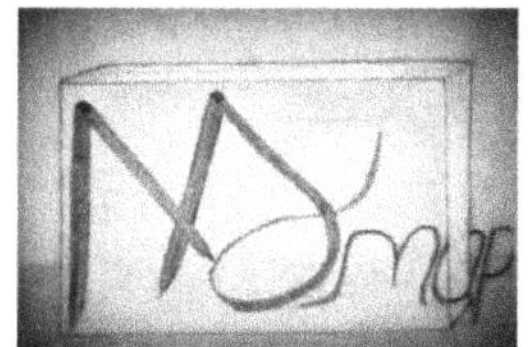

Mwanaka Media and Publishing Pvt Ltd,
Chitungwiza, Zimbabwe
*
Creativity, Wisdom, and Beauty

Publisher: *Mmap*
Mwanaka Media and Publishing Pvt Ltd
24 Svosve Road, Zengeza 1
Chitungwiza, Zimbabwe
mwanaka@yahoo.com
mwanaka13@gmail.com
https://www.mmapublishing.org
www.africanbookscollective.com/publishers/mwanaka-media-and-publishing
https://facebook.com/MwanakaMediaAndPublishing/

Distributed in and outside N. America by African Books Collective
orders@africanbookscollective.com
www.africanbookscollective.com

ISBN: 978-1-77933-150-2
EAN: 9781779331502

DISCLAIMER
All views expressed in this publication are those of the author and do not necessarily reflect the views of *Mmap*.

Table of Contents

Introduction

The three Ps of art: Poetry, Painting and Photography are conjoined with essays in this artistic offering that deals with what it means to be a poet, what constitute a poem, art, art forms, content, and the poet's vocation. It consists of 33 poems, 40 paintings, 7 essays, 10 photographs and an artist statement. Borrowing from the statement by Robert Duncan that poetry comes from God, and twisting it to mean that anything that comes from God and has a life of its own is a god, the poet here becomes a god. He is a god in the form of Adam who is beholden to the earth. He knows there is no heaven for him, so through poetry he creates a heaven for him and his readers using words, images, metaphors, light, lines, circles, space and photography. The book also investigates ghosts in all sorts of forms, from the hallucinatory ghosts to realistic ghosts and irritants. The poetry is driven by the storyteller's eye thus he used the prose narrative form, spinning story strands here and tales there. The poet's obsession with natural elements like the light, the sun, the moon, the wind, the clouds, and the water pervades the book and are at the heart of the poet's painterly journey, as he uses the natural elements to create images, sometimes institutions. Most of the paintings come from his series of abstract paintings on meditations. He uses circles, lines, colour, light to compose images that are imbued with myth, silence and presences (absences). In the poem, *This is not the light of finding you*, he gives us an idea of what he is wrestling with in his art, *"Writing presences, absences, immanence, exigencies, impermanence, as poems that writes permanence on the lines of light that collects in the greys of his head like leftover dreams."* His photography tackles a gamut of issues, from the cityscapes of Pretoria, Johannesburg and Harare, the death of Nyajezi River through siltation and global warming, the dark luminous light of night's fall, birds, trees, the hustling for a living in the streets of Chitungwiza… This book can be taken as an art exhibition at the boundary of 4 disciplines because of its multidisciplinary nature or it can be viewed from the perspective of each of the 4 art disciplines/forms used.

Diagramatologically unleashed

Anderson (1997) stated, generally, "Diagrams are pictorial, yet abstract representation of information, and maps, line, graphs, bar chats, engineering blueprints, and architect's sketches are all examples of diagrams." There are 4 main types of diagrams; vertical, horizontal, matrix and creative…it is the mishmash of these types of diagrams that I interrogate in this collection of paintings in this book representing concepts, ideas, constructions, relations, data, anatomy… The other words for diagrams are schematic, drawing, graphic, plate, scheme, visual, table, schema, cutaway, perspective… then there is issues of how to diagram a sentence, essay, story…..

The circle is one of the most prevalent diagrams you will find in this collection. A circle is a round shaped figure that has no corners or edges, and then there is a radius, diameter (I remember these lines from my poem on love, *What really happened to them*

"Love with walls, lines and rules, love build on an epicenter
And if the diameter of a love song is longer than the melody of its existence,
Will the song remain unresolved?"

And then the formulae for circumference and area of a circle. There are semi-circles, quarter circles, part circles… there is the arc of the circle etc…. Full circles represent totality, femininity, a symbol of the sun, moon, wholeness, original perfection, the self, the infinite, eternity, timelessness, all cyclic movements, God (according to Hermes Trismegistus, God is a circle whose centre is everywhere and whose circumference is nowhere), Evil spirits (in the movie, The Twin, circular forms are said to lead to the sacrificial rock, pagan beliefs, human imperfections, bile of hurt, infinite swing of the pendulum. People who got the circles when the shapes were handed down are destroyers of all virtues. They are here and they are there). What shape was given to you? I will write a poem someday about this. A half circle is sensitive, vulnerable and easily influenced like the soul, an ongoing growing, experience and passing expression of the true self…then there is the circle of life, social circles, goddess circle, spiral circles, inner circle *(a la la, la la, li long long, standing across the room I see you smile)*, support circles….

And the line is another useful composition tool I employ in these paintings. A line is a long, narrow mark or band, a length of cord, rope, wire, or other materials serving a particular purpose. Other words for a line are dash, rule, bar…then there is calculation of line, vertex, function, (a line adds information to a diagram, it follows a plot command that produce a graph). The plot plots the points, not the line. In art line, a line diagram (drawing) is any image that consists of distinct straight lines or curves placed against a background, without gradations in shade or hue to represent two dimensional or three dimensional objects. Line art can use lines of different colours. Line is one of the most important compositional elements in these artworks, used to define shapes and figures, but to also indicate motion, emotion and other elements… They are many types of lines in these paintings, from thick, thin, horizontal, dotted, circles, vertical, zigzag, diagonal, curly, curved, spiral….

My art uses the diagrams, could be circles, boxes, buildings, blocks, rectangles, triangular, cubes, prisms…, and mix them with the creative elements of art like colour, light, plot, line, to create shapes. Words are shapes, letters are shapes, circles are shapes, that which can be seen is a shape. That's the basics of visual art. Visual literature is the most powerful element. Why diagrams? In my O level studies at Nyatate secondary school, Nyanga, Zimbabwe, in my first form we were introduced to technical drawing, a subject I excelled in. Those elements we were taught for 2 years stayed with me all through my life. And at A level I studied mathematics, and diagrams were part of my visual narrative, even though it was technical. I remember my A level teacher, Mr Chinamasa describing the line of asymptote as a line that approaches the x or y axis lines but never really touches it, making it more understandable visually by saying it's like the way a man approaches a woman. Can we never really touch the woman? Even though in later life I gravitated towards the arts, you can still see the science in my drawings, that is mixed with symbolism (mostly religious and or spiritual) thus these drawings are conceptual representation of larger human, spatial and spiritual issues.

Artist statement

My work takes the nature of interactive, collaborative and the multidisciplinary. I work across several art fields, including among others literary (fictions, novels, essays poetry, play, short stories, songs…), musical (composition, singing, reciting, mbira, marimba, keyboards, a little guitar…), and visual (drawings, paintings, photography, collages, mixed media, installation etc…) I am interested in connection, convergence, community and cooperation, following disparate sometimes disfigured experiences, seeing how they can come together or shy away from each other to create new wholes.

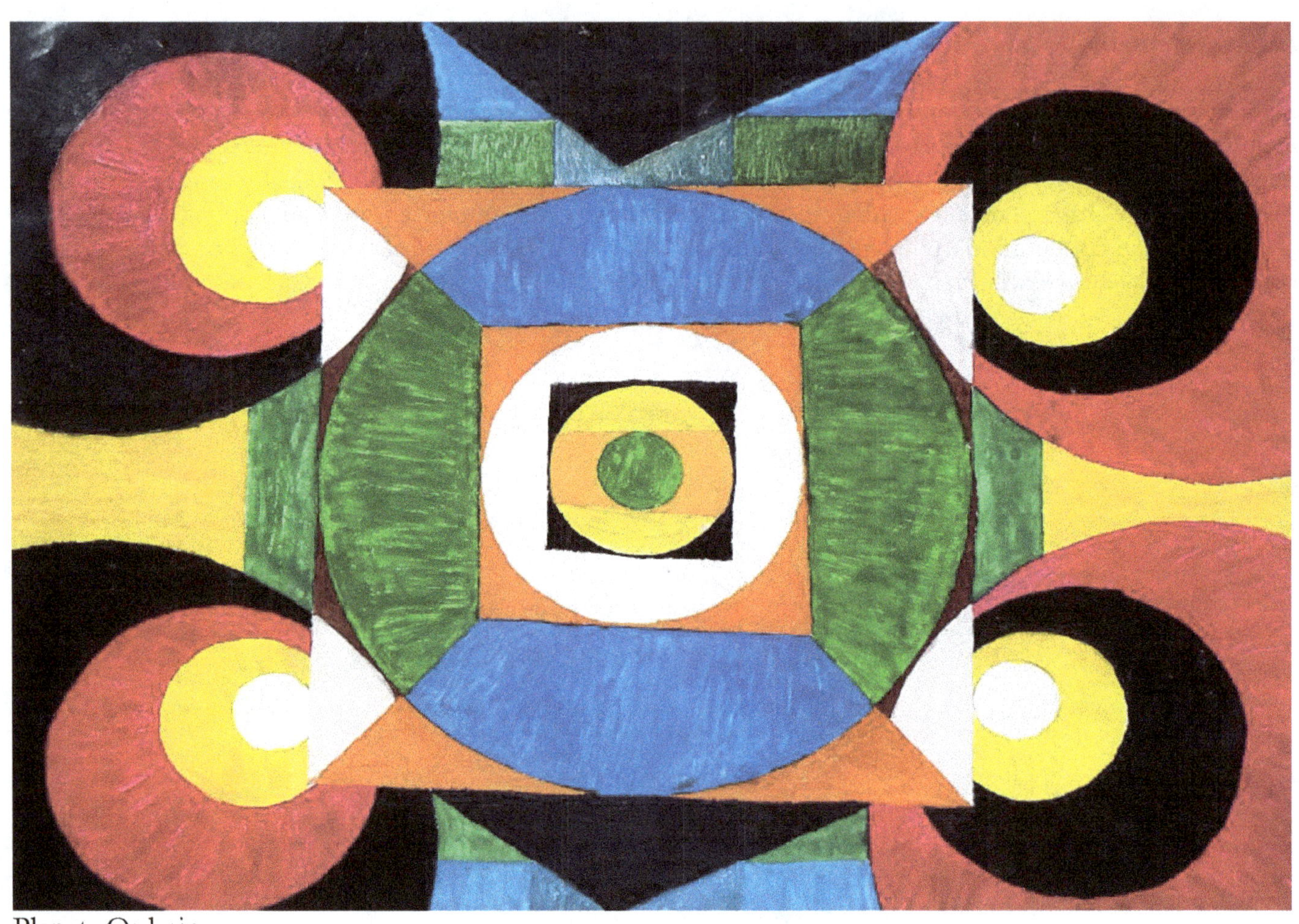

Planets Ordering
Acrylics and watercolors on paper
50 cm by 65 cm
2023

The shape of light

Breathing life into spaces
And giving these spaces scars
Vapourous mists, variegated fields
Architectural mimefields of colours
Setting up an intense becoming
A whole apparatus of revelations
Omissions, conflations and protections
Striving for a life that has no physical shape
By borrowing from physical lines
That are a presence without narrative
Where form is emptiness, emptiness is form
And the shape of light,
Is the area between form and emptiness?
Where relationships between colours, forms, concepts
And materiality are themes in themselves, of
Transcendent humans in unholy suits

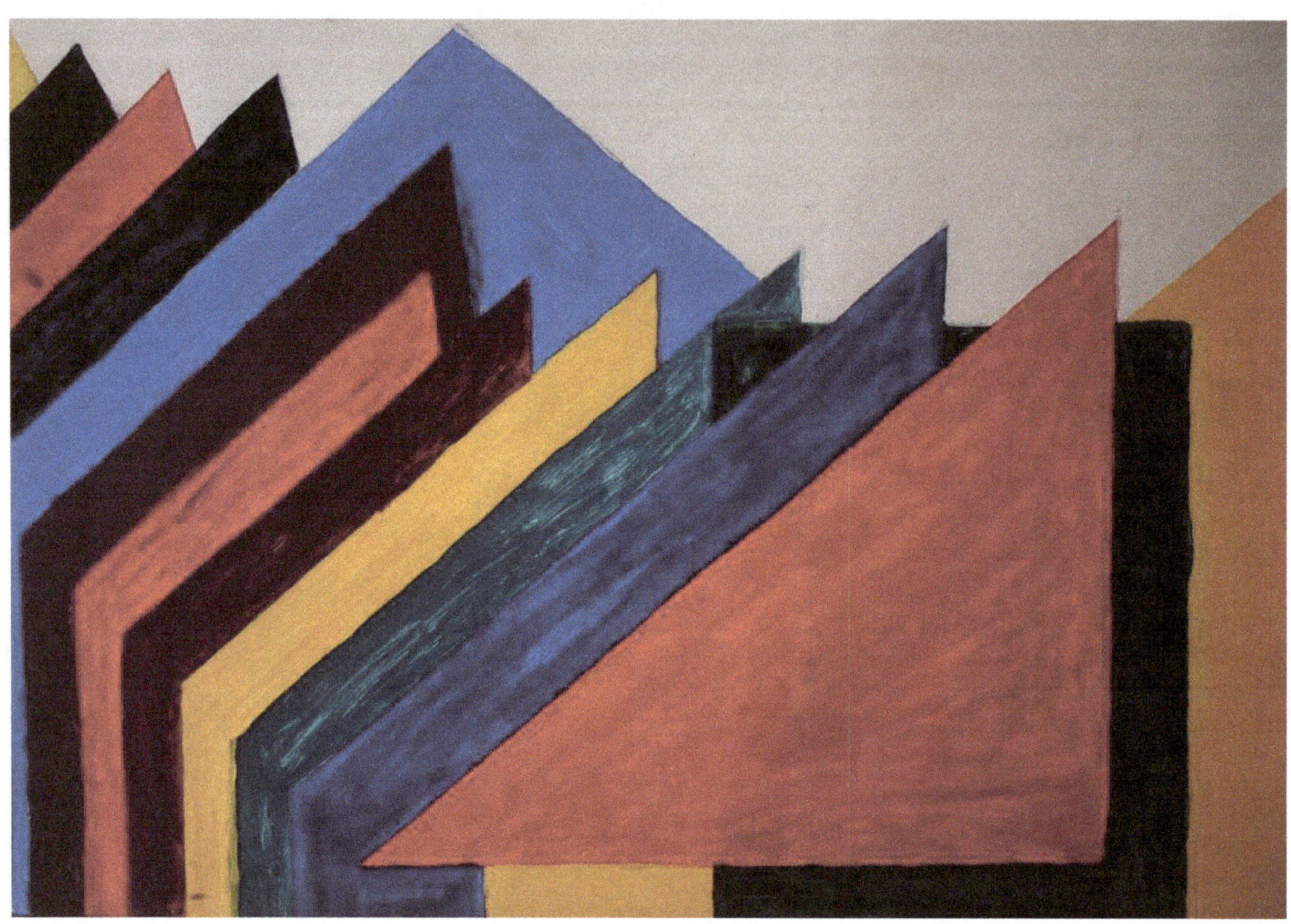

The shape of light
Acrylics on white board
Size: 42cm by 59.4cm
Year: 2022

He Thinks He is a Poet

Cap~~ital~~ lock~~s~~ T ~~comma duration slash he removed the first comma~~ it's a word that ends with i *and a full stop*
We forgot to ask it *comma* to question mark a name *comma*
Cap the M in the word that ends with a *comma* who is that *question mark*
He thinks he is a poet *semi-colon* Language picker *comma* a name *comma* misnomer *comma* a wordyard *comma*
vowels *comma* the sixth vowel *dash* consonants *comma* syntaxes *full stop*
Language man *dash* before the information age killed his fire *full stop*
Oh *exclamation mark* suffering cheating object *ellipses*

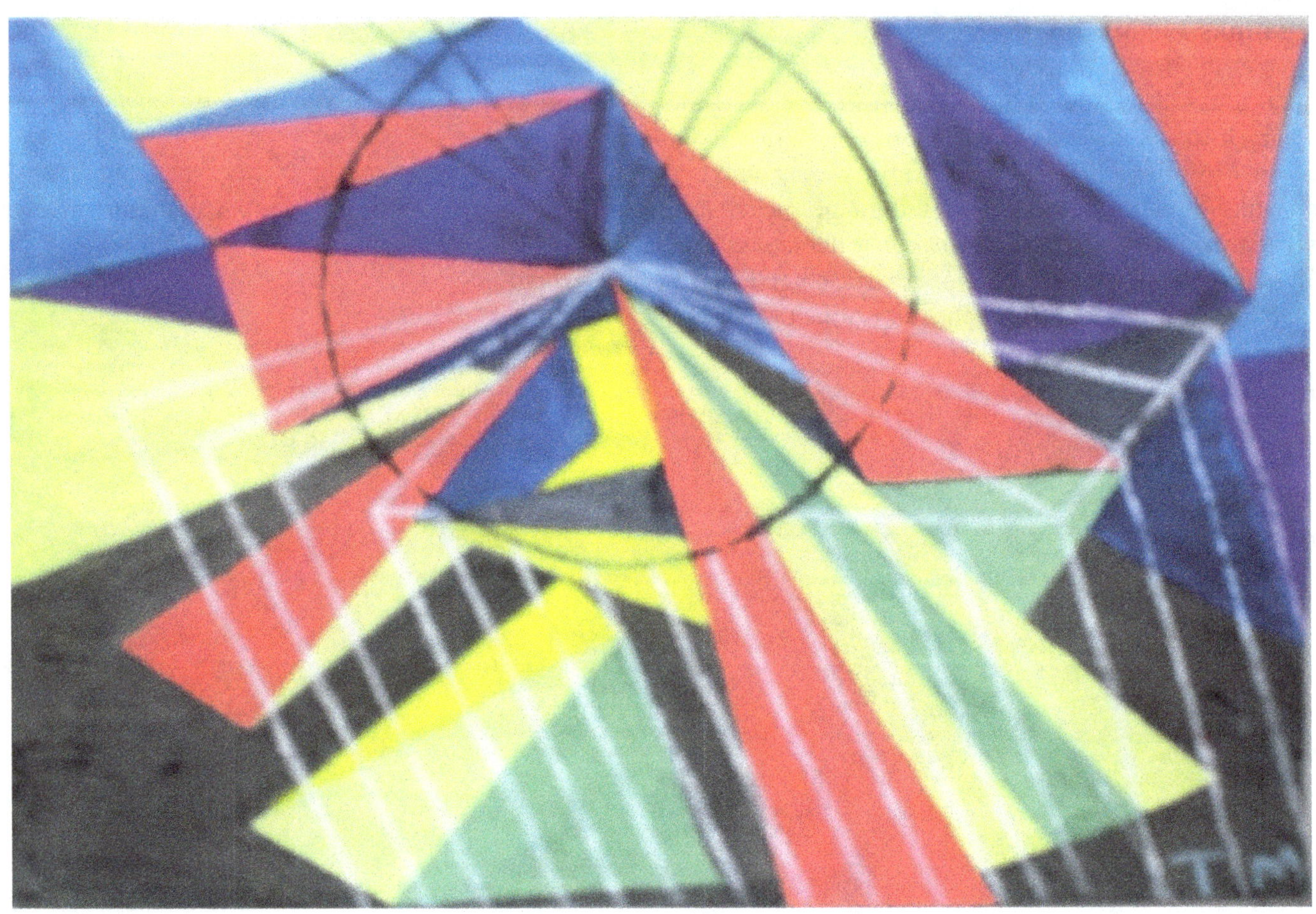

The rising sun
Acrylics, watercolours and charcoal on fabriano paper
Size 29.7cm by 42cm
Year: 2022

The pointless want to care

That moment when I want to post my photos on facebook. That moment when I want everyone on facebook to like everything I am posting like the hot word 'woke' is awake. That moment when I am furious at everyone on facebook, as in fuck you, whole- for not liking everything I am posting. Where am I without this, me waiting, holding onto my phone like Eve to the apple, waiting for your likes, waiting and waiting… That moment when i want to scream at you all for not liking my posts- a day has passed by without any likes. This pointless want to care is now the indicator, it fattens me.

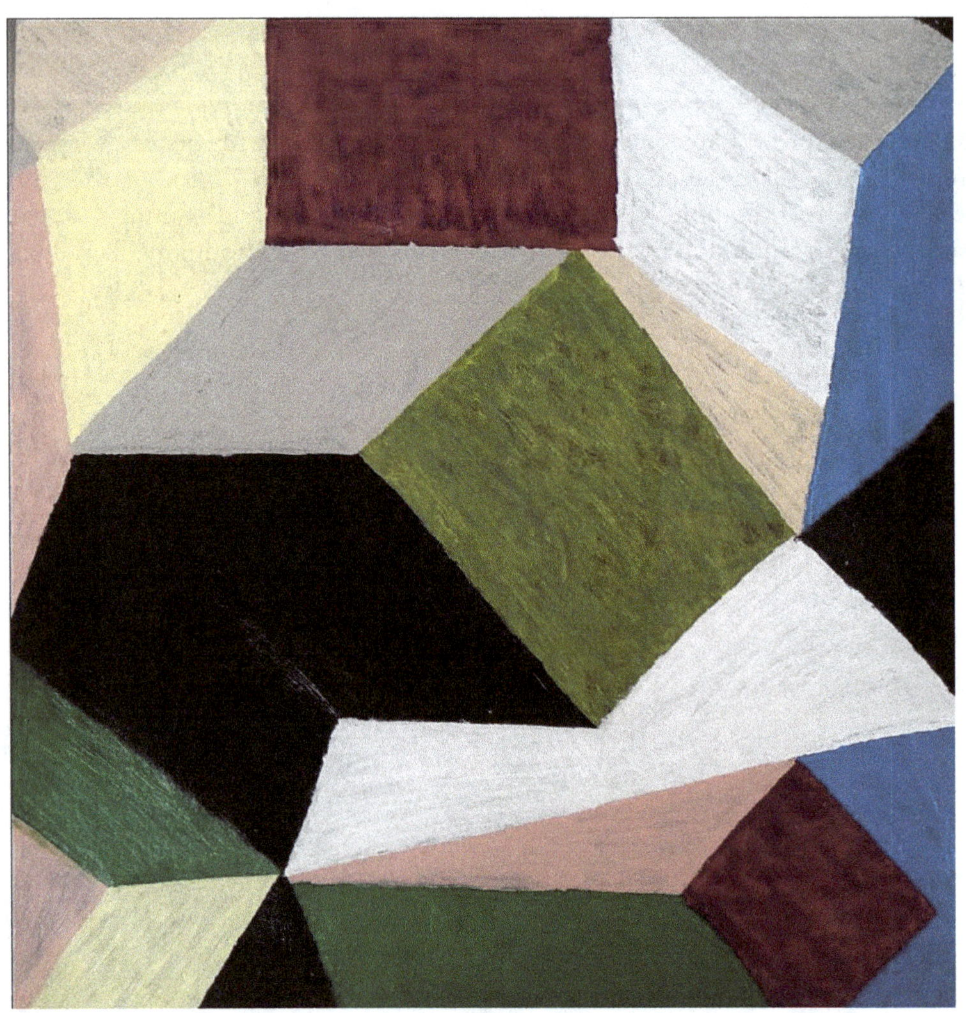

Angular anger
Watercolours and Acrylics on fabriano paper
Size: 42cm by 59.4cm
2023

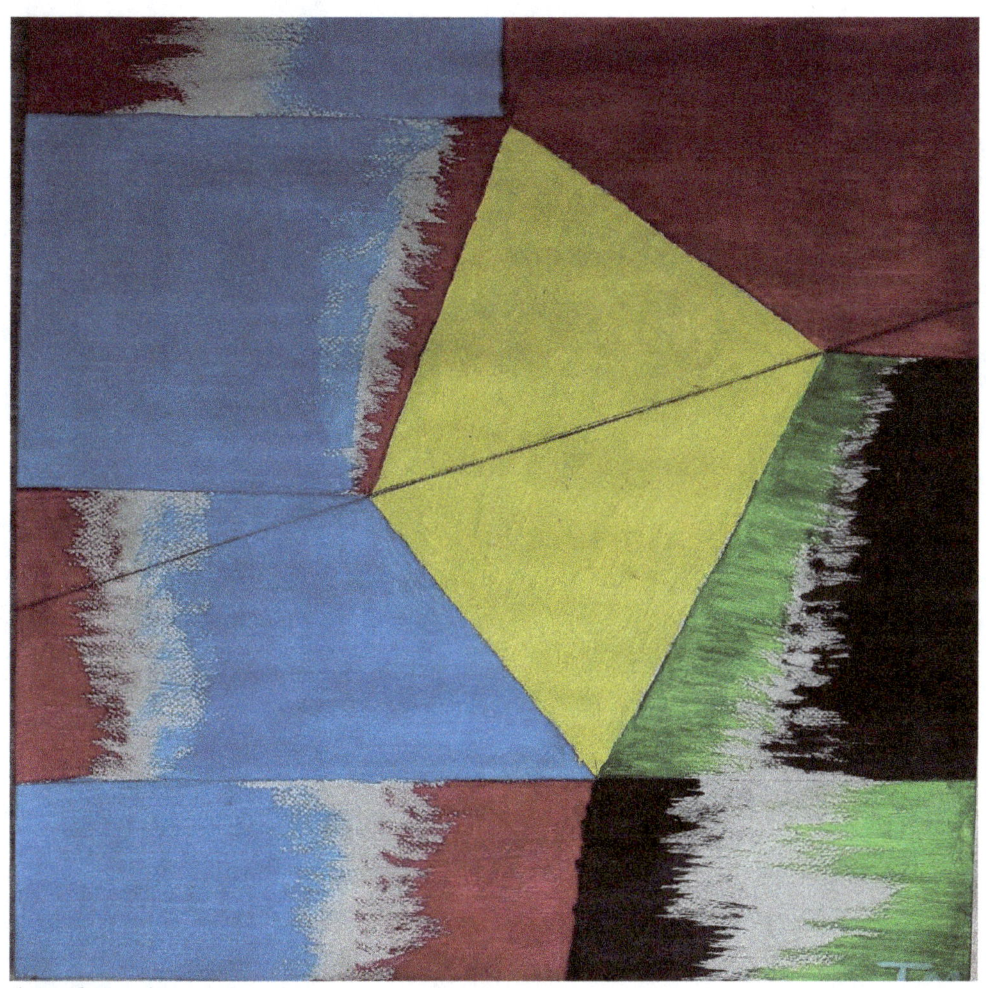

Angular pain
Acrylics, watercolours and charcoal on fabriano paper
Size: 42cm by 59.4cm
Year: 2022

After five years

After seeing her, after five years, after losing her sister who connected us, I told her there was no need for us to talk to each other again, to see each other again. That I had seen her for me and that the next time she comes home I won't be there. She says 'its ok'. She tells me where I have stopped talking to her, seeing her, is where she would rest. And I thought something must be wrong with her or that she was in love. I guess it's not only scientists who want their hypothesis answered!

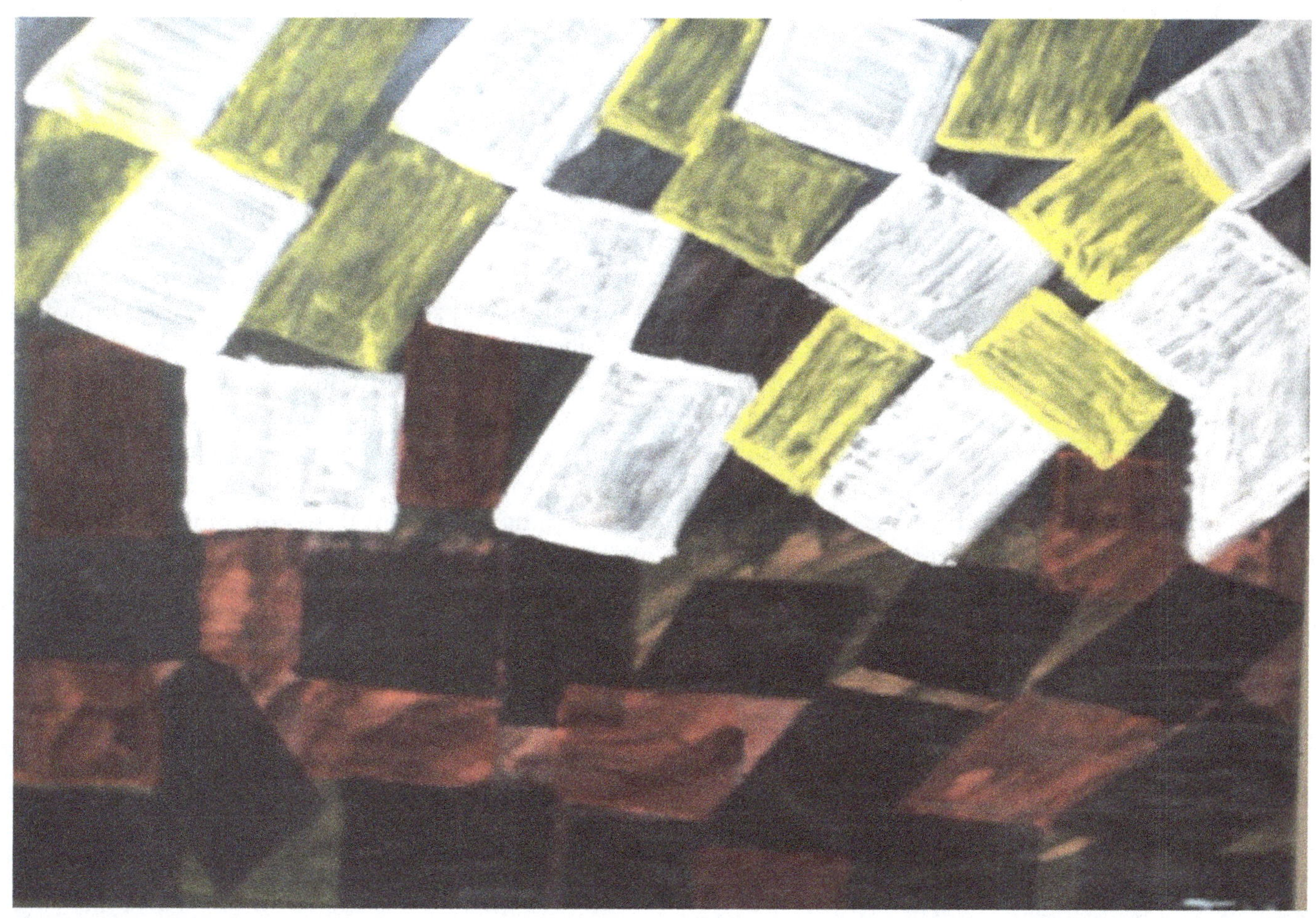

Boxed in
Acrylics on canvass
Size: 45.7cm by 60.9cm
Year 2022

Are you watching me?
For Nicholas Tachiveyi

I have made a goodbye with you when I saw your face, thin in death, at the first viewing before the short-long trek to your naval home. Now I think maybe you are watching me. From 9 pm to 3 am we got stuck in Jemedza mountain's trails on our way to your resting place. Cheshumba mountain's lions laughed at us, as we struggled to cross the sacred pools. *"Pamudzimundateura is sacred, it's you who knows it, kwakandibvuma is sacred, it's you who knows it. Its only you, you, you who knows this,"* James Chimombe had belted song and sorrow in 1990 about this place as he faced a toneless nightfall, before he puked out a failure among the living. Now, Jemedza Mountain is swielding its sword at us to the point I asked others if they thought you could really be watching us, punishing us. With the night's decline, at the graveyard's eulogy, I am lost for the words to the point I hoped you were not watching me, wrestling with this suddenness of loss. I couldn't view your face again as they took another peep at you for the last time like that saying if you are going to bury something, do not look at it, chances it would bite you in the eyes. I can't think of you watching what I am doing or thinking or feeling, but you not saying anything to let me know you see me. As your casket disappears into the hole, hand to hand, we still the feelings in funeral dirges as everything blooms, disappears, and reappears in the misty Njanja's torn clothes of rain.

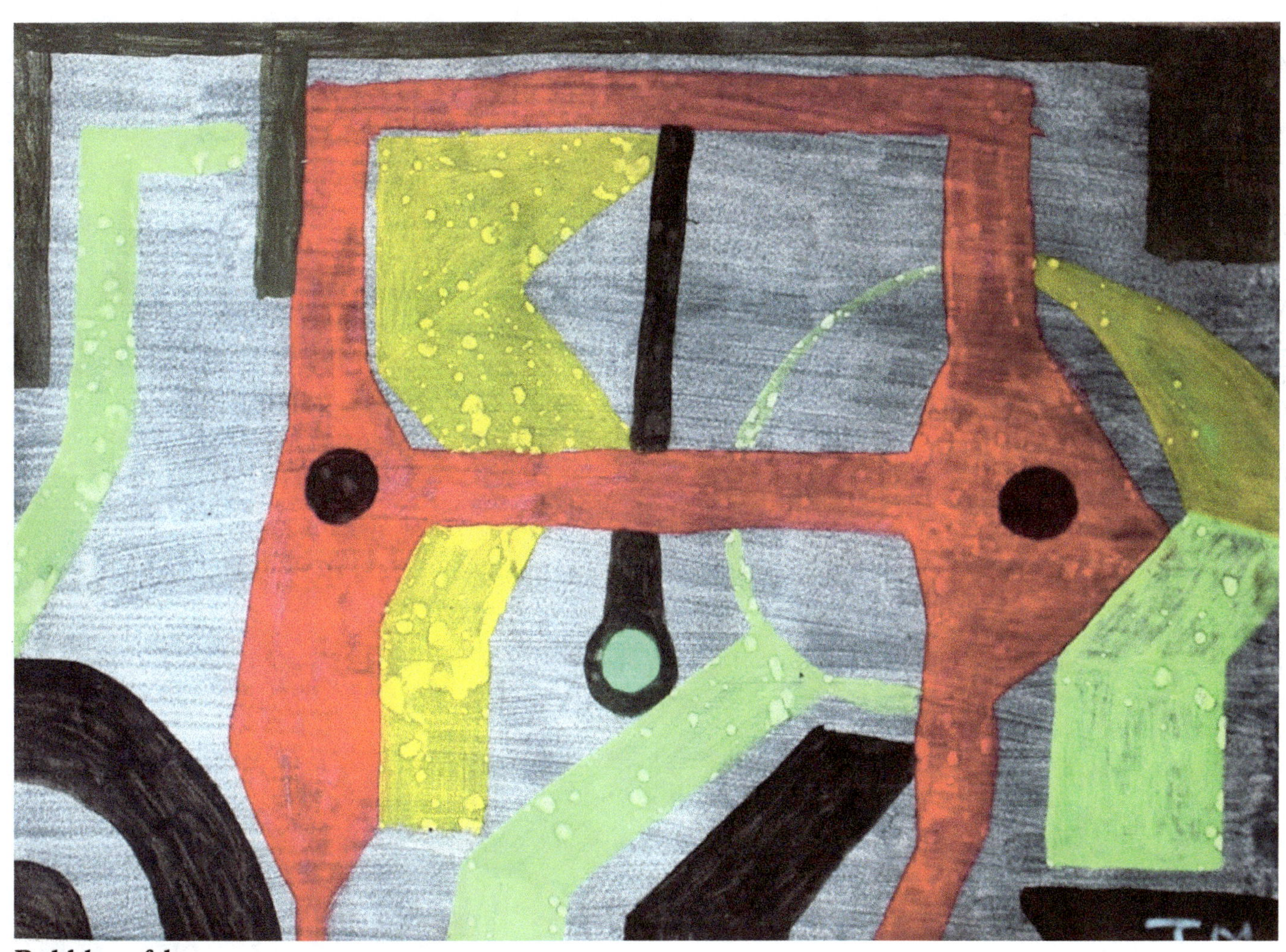

Bubbles of love
Watercolous, acrylics on fabriano paper
Size: 42cm by 59.4cm
2022

Meditation series #1

Airforce blue is the origin story of this universe
Grey blocks of dark energy flows downwards
And some grey energies commutes bello horizontes to the universe
Double blocks of white matter hold this universe together
A yellow board of life encircles the universe's largest earth
White Circular earths are lineal between the grey blocks
Syncopate circles cinges the middles of these blocks like buttons,
In blue planets, yellow planets, red planets, each in its own gradient
Gravity giving to each planet a moving tangent
It is a universe of colours, form, composition,
Circles, lines and blocks-
sometimes forming human torsos

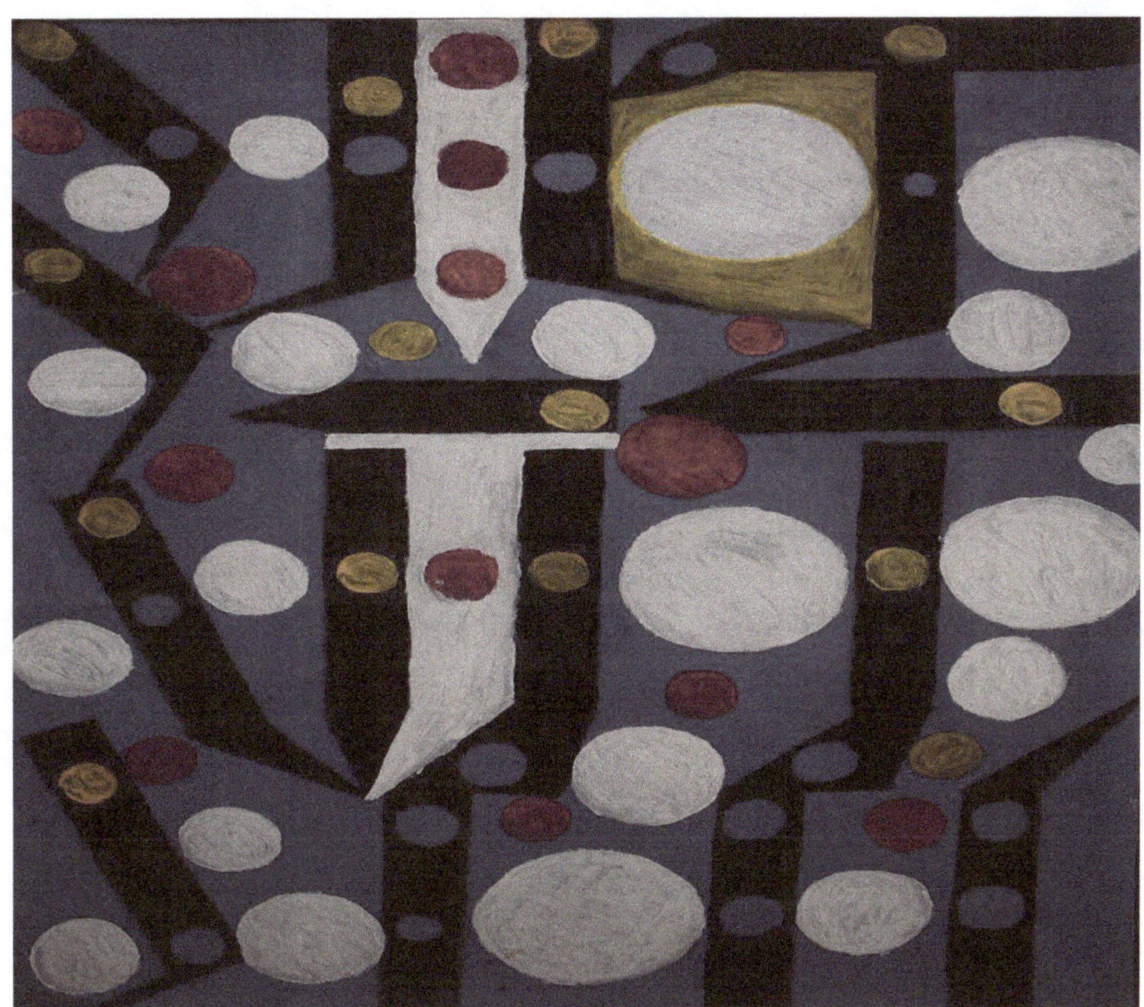

Meditation series #1
Acrylics on canvass
Size: 42cm by 59.4cm
Year: 2022

1 Corinthians 13 vs 11-12

11. When I was younger, and to erase myself from blame, I would forget or lie, forget or lie, forget or lie… I would lie about my name, about my birthmarks, about my shadows. Forgetting would take over my name to recover what name was hidden inside my own. And when I was a teen, and to erase myself from blame, I would make strangers uncomfortable, I would make old people uncomfortable, I would make my parents uncomfortable, and then overcompensate by hugging them, that giddy feeling of power and burden was like when my first lover curved her tastes into me, combing for me the paths to new homes. But when I became a man I put away the *Tena koe e Meri* that was sung like a private anthem. Now there is still more tea to be drunk!

12. For now we see the windowed rivers, and face to face they frighten us enough. Now I know in part, it's that time to speak of love again, but then I also know that someone has to stand around and watch the cattle all day….

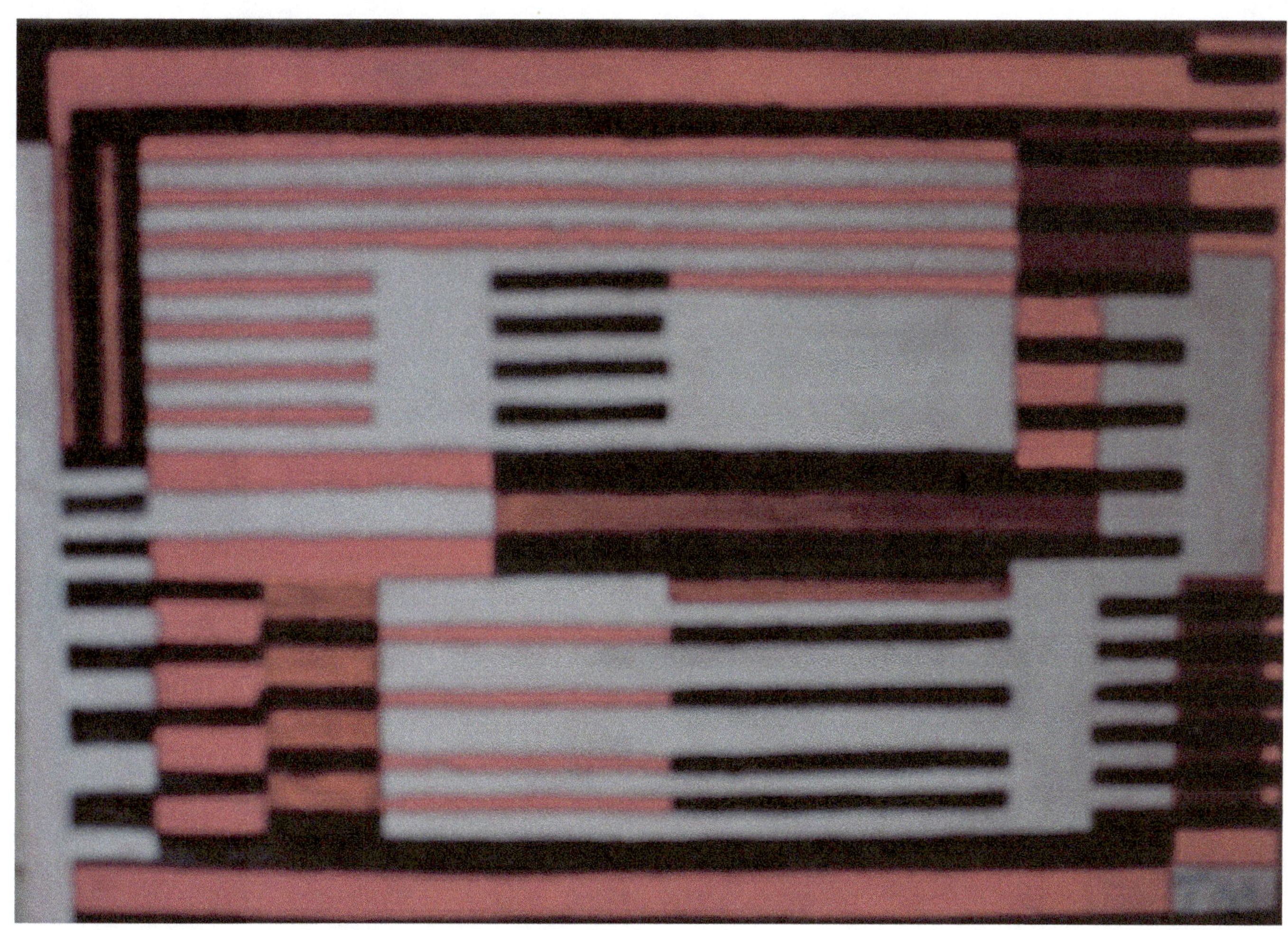

Centimental
Acrylics on canvass
Size: 42cm by 59.4cm
2022

I write what I write

I write very simple poems, sometimes, sometimes I write difficult poems. But when you read them, never, I said never, assume I had written them for you. I wrote them that way because I simply had to write them that way. I had to do that because there is no other curve of the horizon that could house me. You didn't ask me to write them for you. So, never come to me with this and that rule, or advice on why I must write poems this way or that way because if you paint over a glass window it ceases to be a window, but it would never become wheat, maize or rice…

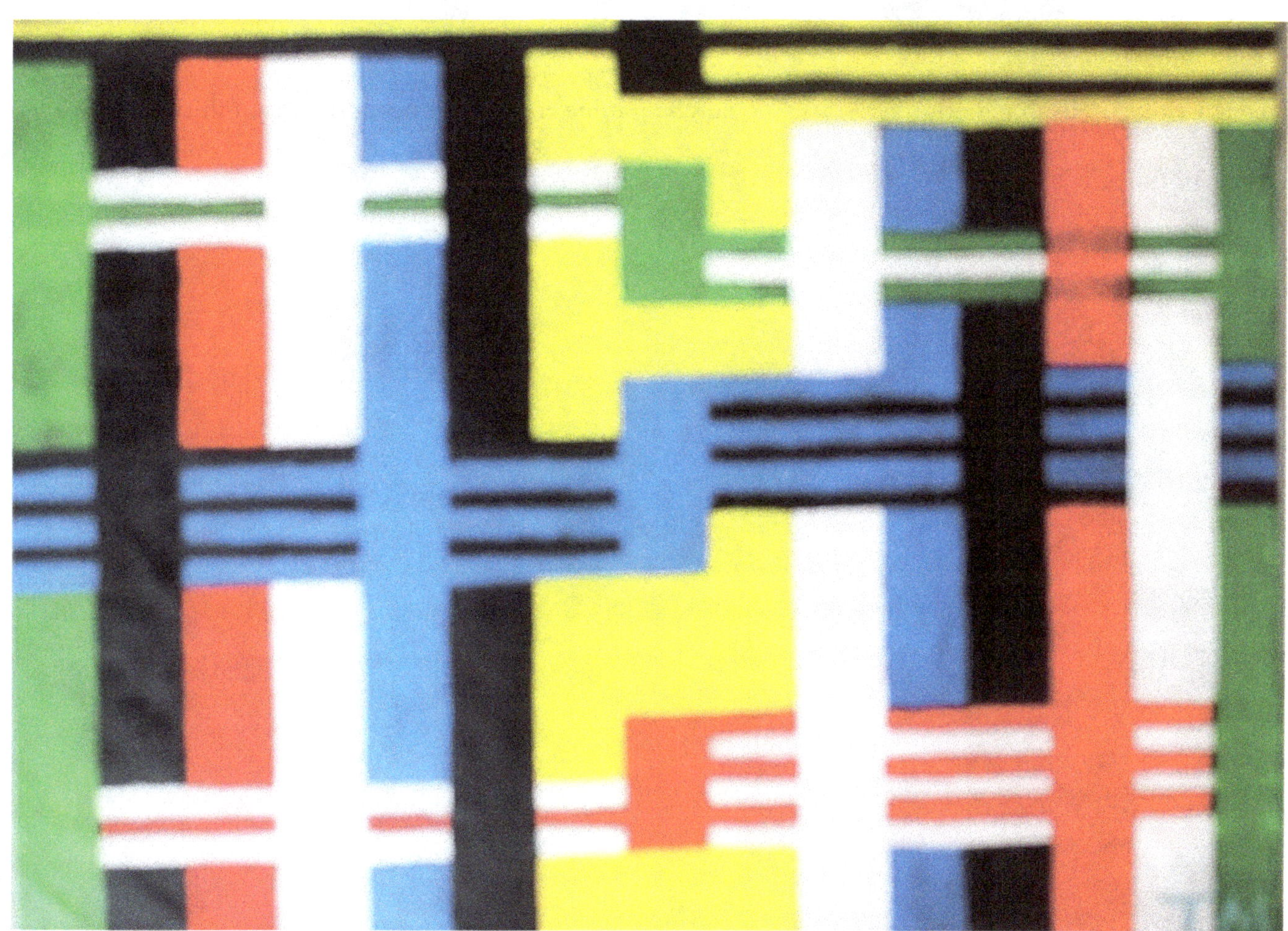

Still Centimental
Acrylics on canvass
Size: 42cm by 59.4cm
2022

Someday

Someday I woke up in somebody's arms, a hand clutching mine, and, "do I need to tell you the whole story?"

Chant *yes* 10 times....

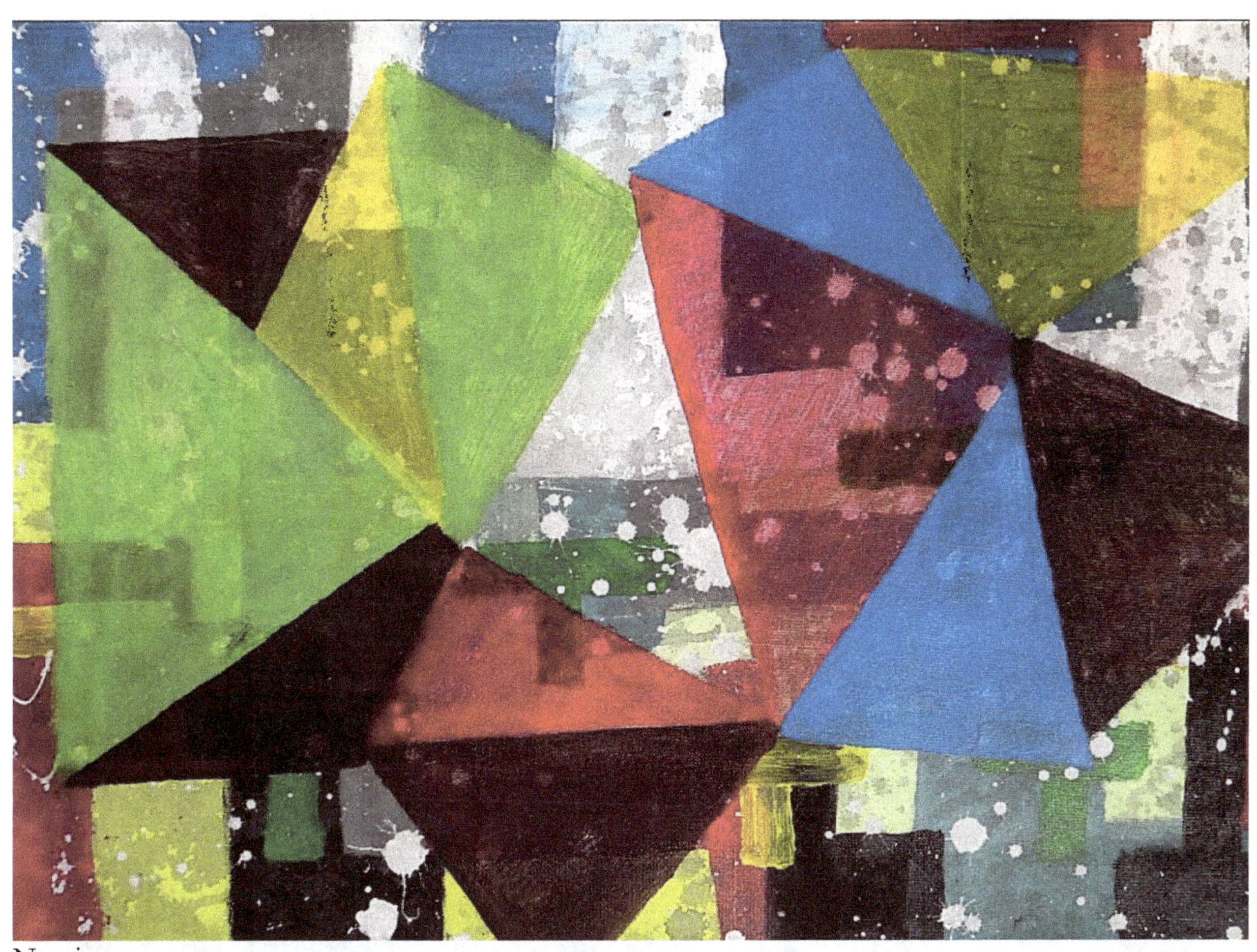

Naming
Acrylics and water colours on canvas
Size: 42cm by 59.4cm
2023

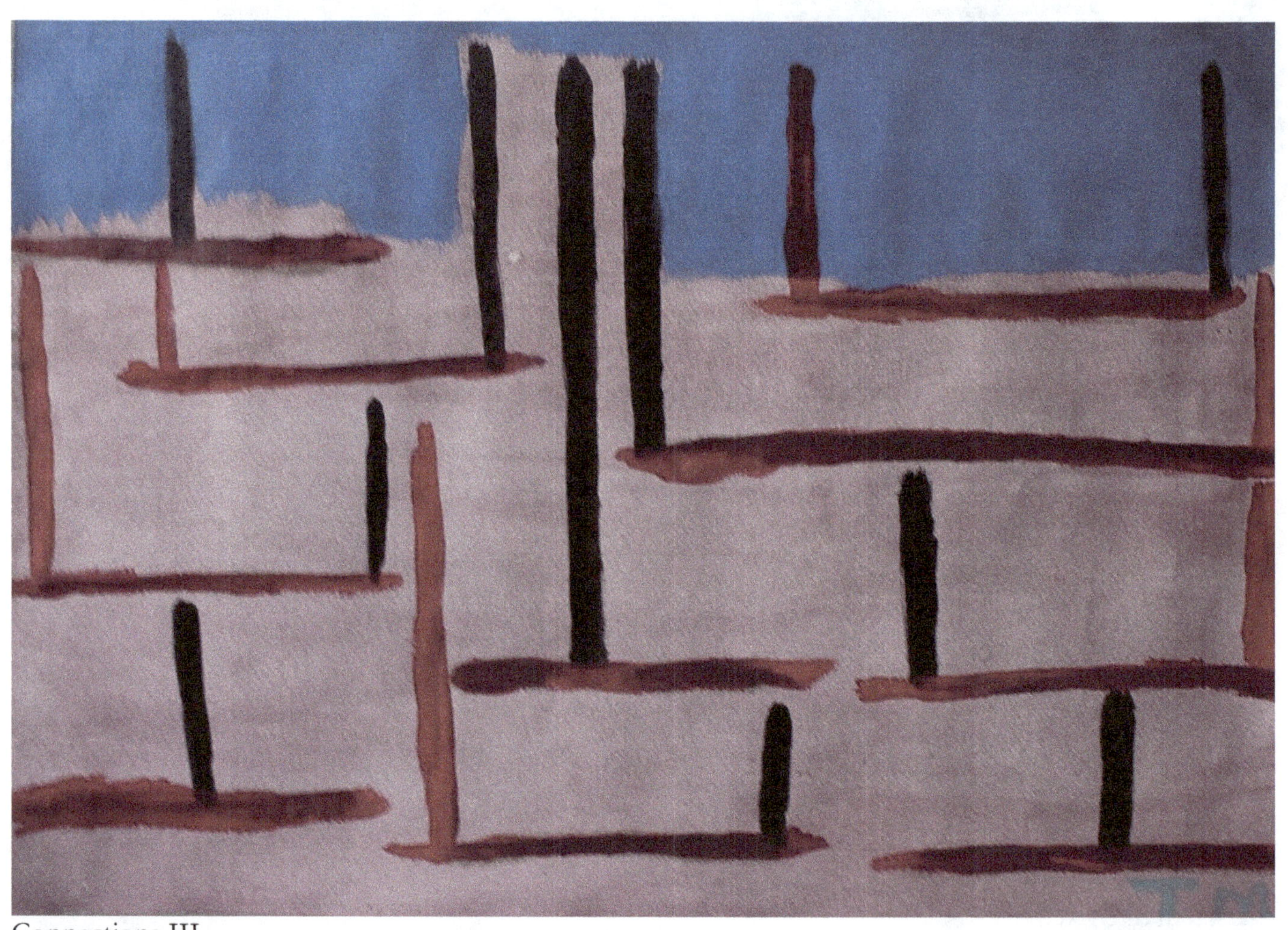

Connections III
Watercolours, acrylics on fabriano paper
Size: 42cm by 59.4cm

2022

To show that an Idea has a history in order to reclaim it, by owning Miranda Mellis' Demystifications Series

#1
I am that one time when we kicked, with our bran new school shoes, that oddly shaped rock, all the way home from school. Mom looking at our broken, torn shoes with anger that could only commute with sticks, and us standing far away enough, ready to fly away.

#2
I am that Christmas day when we left the cattle in the bushes and went to the local shops to celebrate with others, only to fail to find our cattle by night's fall. They had wandered away. We were the cattle that slept at the cattle kraal learning to sentence our errant selves by staying away from her sticks. We picked up small stones and turned them into soup in our mouths like that old lady of Chivi Shona proverb.

#3
I am the chewed scents of Harare's early mornings as a night shift Fauwcett security guard in the Kopje area of Harare, learning that night was created by an error of commission in accounting. It was just a few hours, and then it stayed for 8 more hours commissioned to act for mornings, which is night's duty.

#4
I am that 1990s Zimbabwe hustler into mining spots, into Botswana, into Mozambique, sleeping under the pounding rains, thinking the rains would stop and make a tune that I would hear again in my heart. Surely, one does not need a body in heaven, my skins still throb when I remember about the rains.

#5
I am that boy, fresh out of high school trusting nothing else but his pen, that his pen is everything, trusting in the pentametric round terrains of an Eversharp pen.

#6

After everything, after 4 years invoicing and selling cars, cars, cars, at Amtec Motors, until cars are all I thought I hear, I turned my face in the direction I still remembered was where the pen was, heading to the old beginning....

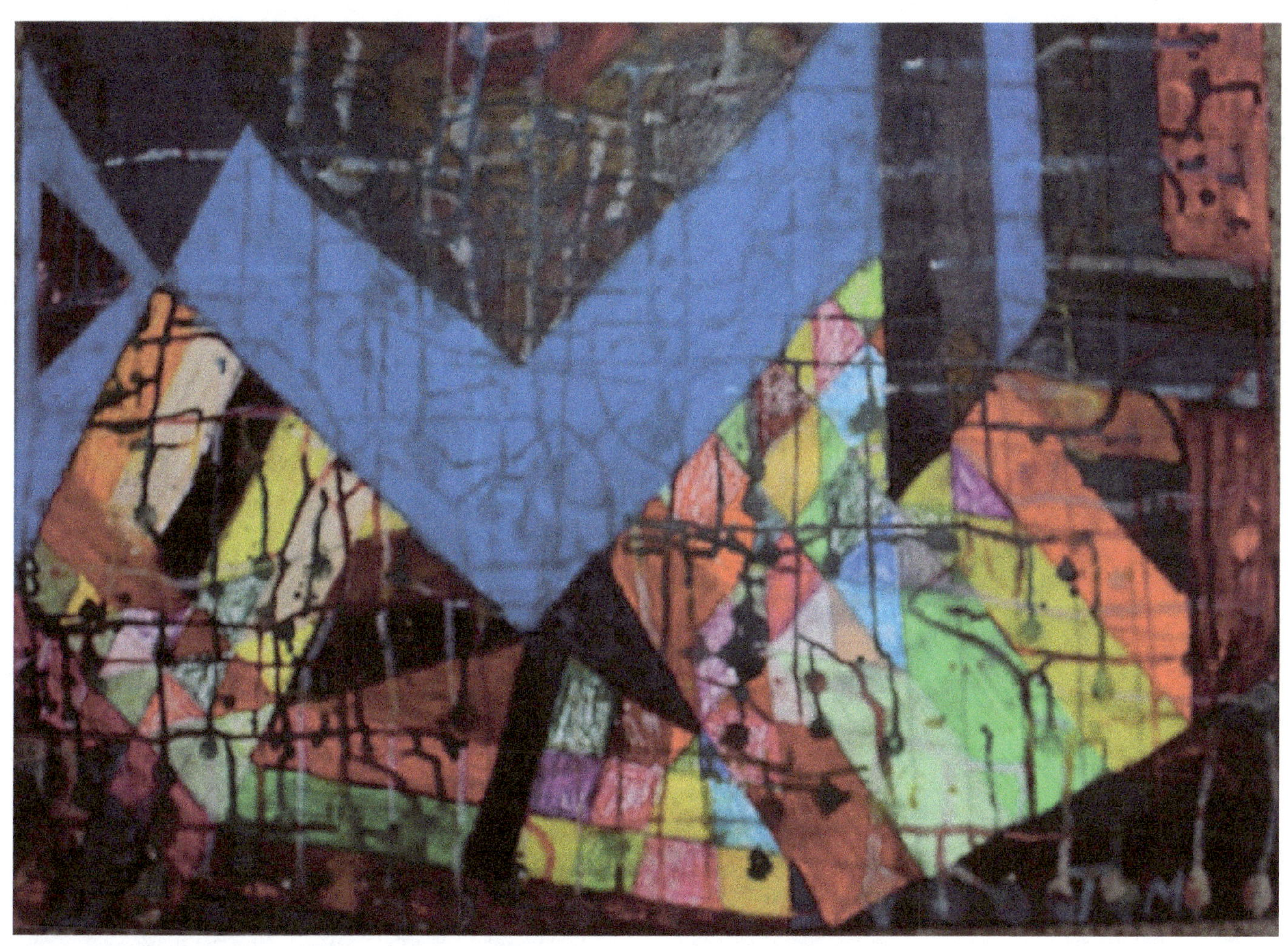

Constructed humans
Acrylics and oil pastels on canvass
50.4cm by 76.2cm
Year 2022

If I am Dreaming

If I dream I am dreaming, yet I am awake, you say *don't dream, don't dream, don't dream*. I shove something Wittgensteinian at you, "we are asleep, our life is like a dream, only in better hours do we wake enough to realize we dream." *Who am I kidding*, you say, *wake up, wake up, wake up*. The wake of the universe beating warmth at my doorstep, my words are useless. I cannot shake myself to consciousness

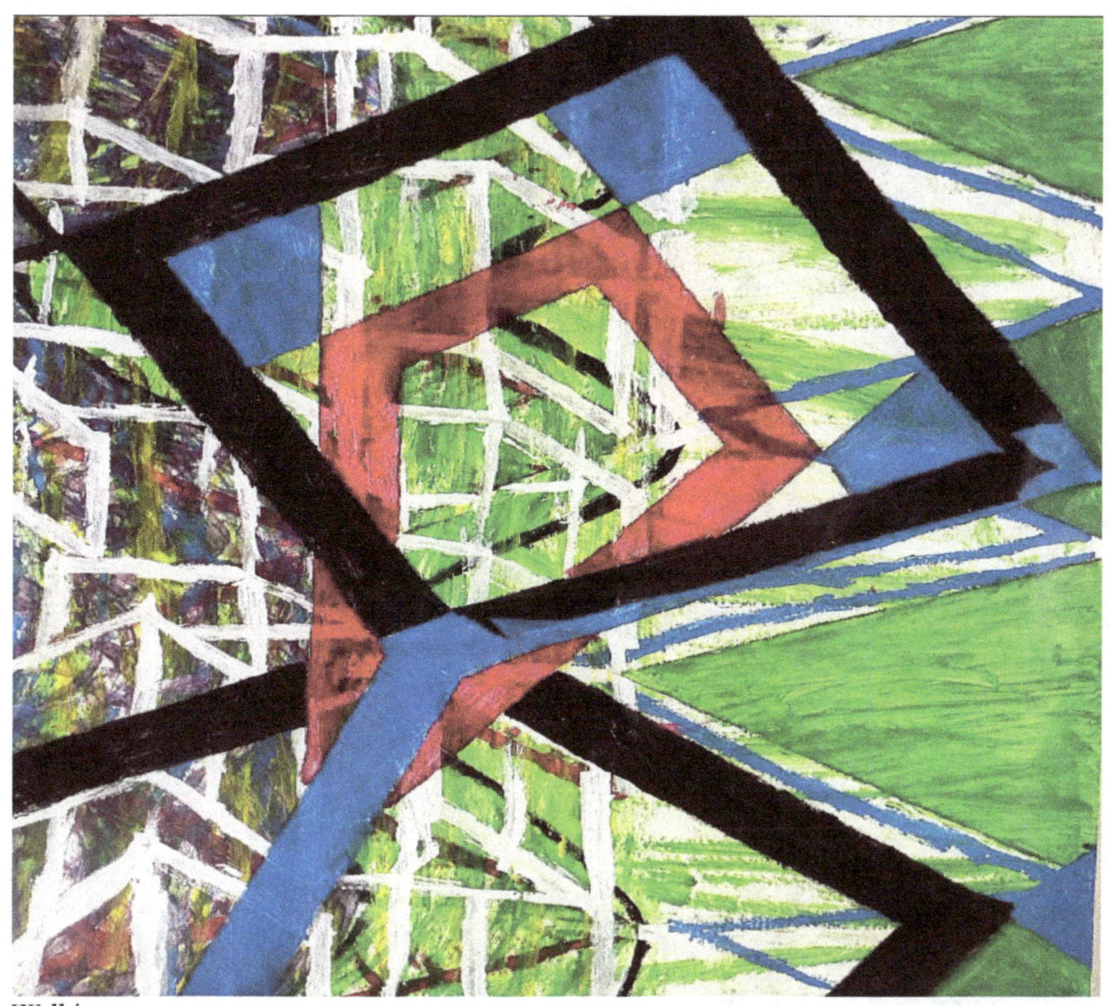

Walking away
Acrylics and watercolours on paper
50cm by 65 cm
2023

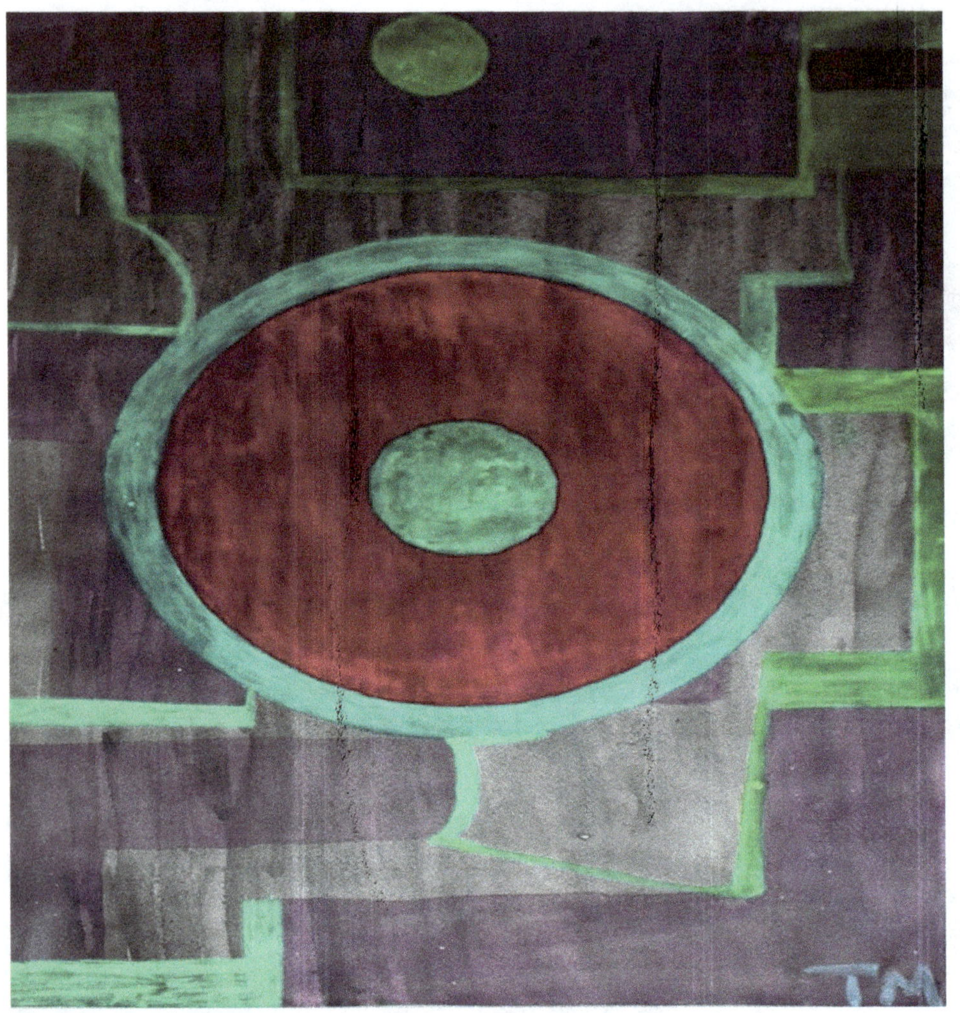

The Green circle
Watercolours, and acrylics on fabriano paper
Size: 42cm by 59.4cm
2022

I never saw them again!

Somewhere in the quiet violence of the 1990s, there was this group of Watch Tower Society bible road preachers, a middle aged man, a pretty slip of a girl, and the vocal young man who I used to have rousing bible discussions with every Saturday. At the end of the discussion I would give them bananas, sometimes apples, or whatever, to eat. And reliable like an assuming hour hand, the next Saturday around 8 am in the morning they will be entering my gates. I had tolerated them first time because I thought I could get inroads with the pretty girl. First days I would ask good questions to their readings and explanations. We would argue, read the bible, promise to do that next Saturday, promise each other heaven and I would give them bananas… I think the middle aged man liked me. Not that way, please! Then when I realized I could never get a moment with the pretty girl, when I was bored by their intent to try to convert me, one Saturday I decided to ask non-controversial questions when they asked me to ask questions. I am like, holding their non-controversial booklets of clichés, where lions and little kids are pictured playing together in heaven, everything is the green of Uganda, the bananas, oranges, berries, cows sleeping on human beds, so I asked them what kind of paper are their sermons printed on. Who wrote the bible? Did they bind the booklets, what kind of binding, who took the cover photographs, are the staples from Germany…they couldn't say God in all the answers, and then I told them I had no bananas to give them that day. I never saw them again!

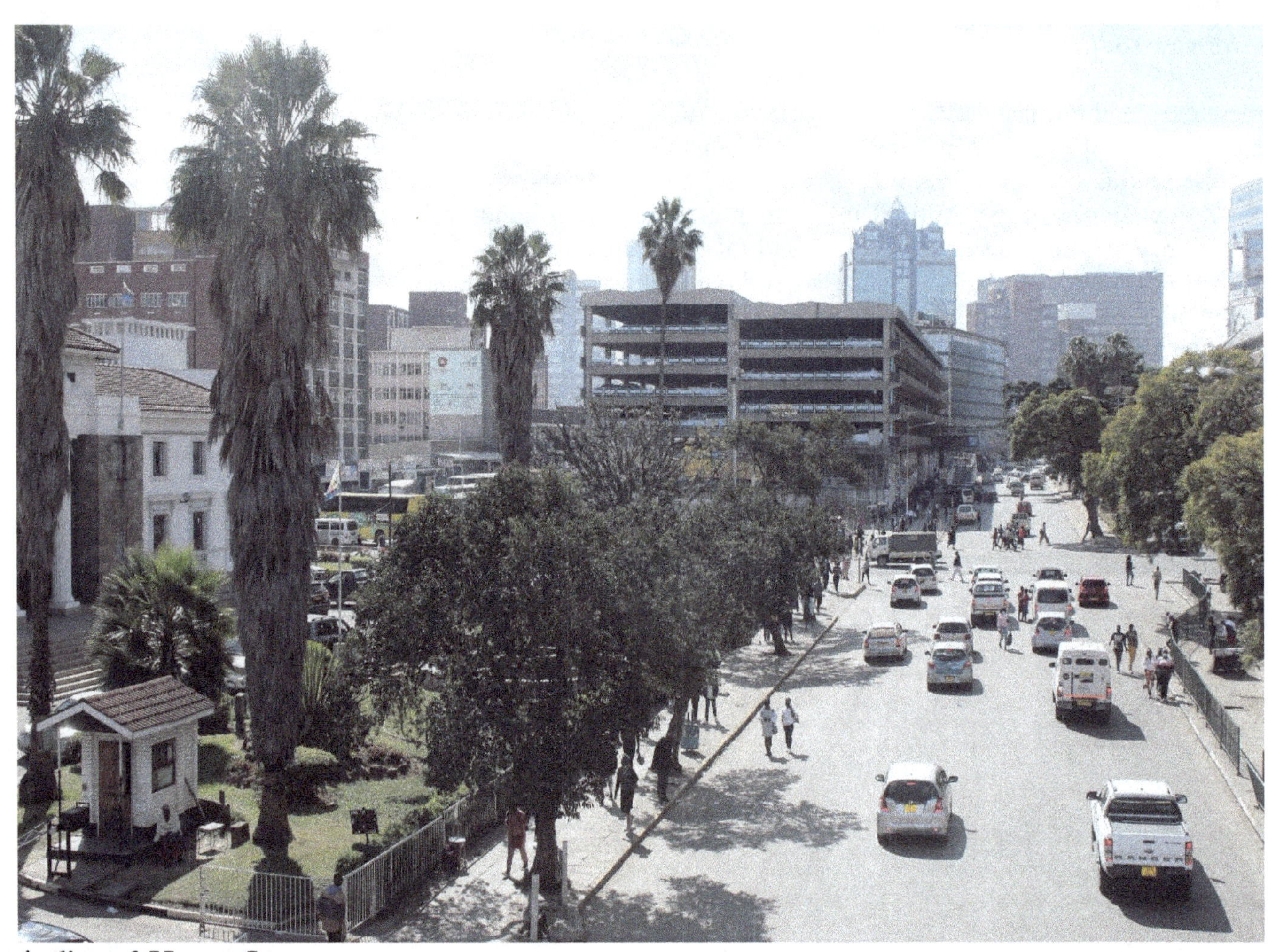

A slice of Harare I,
Digital photography
July 2022

How to control humans

Three worst animals created by humans:
~~Religion~~// ~~Capitalism~~// ~~Weapons~~//
Humans

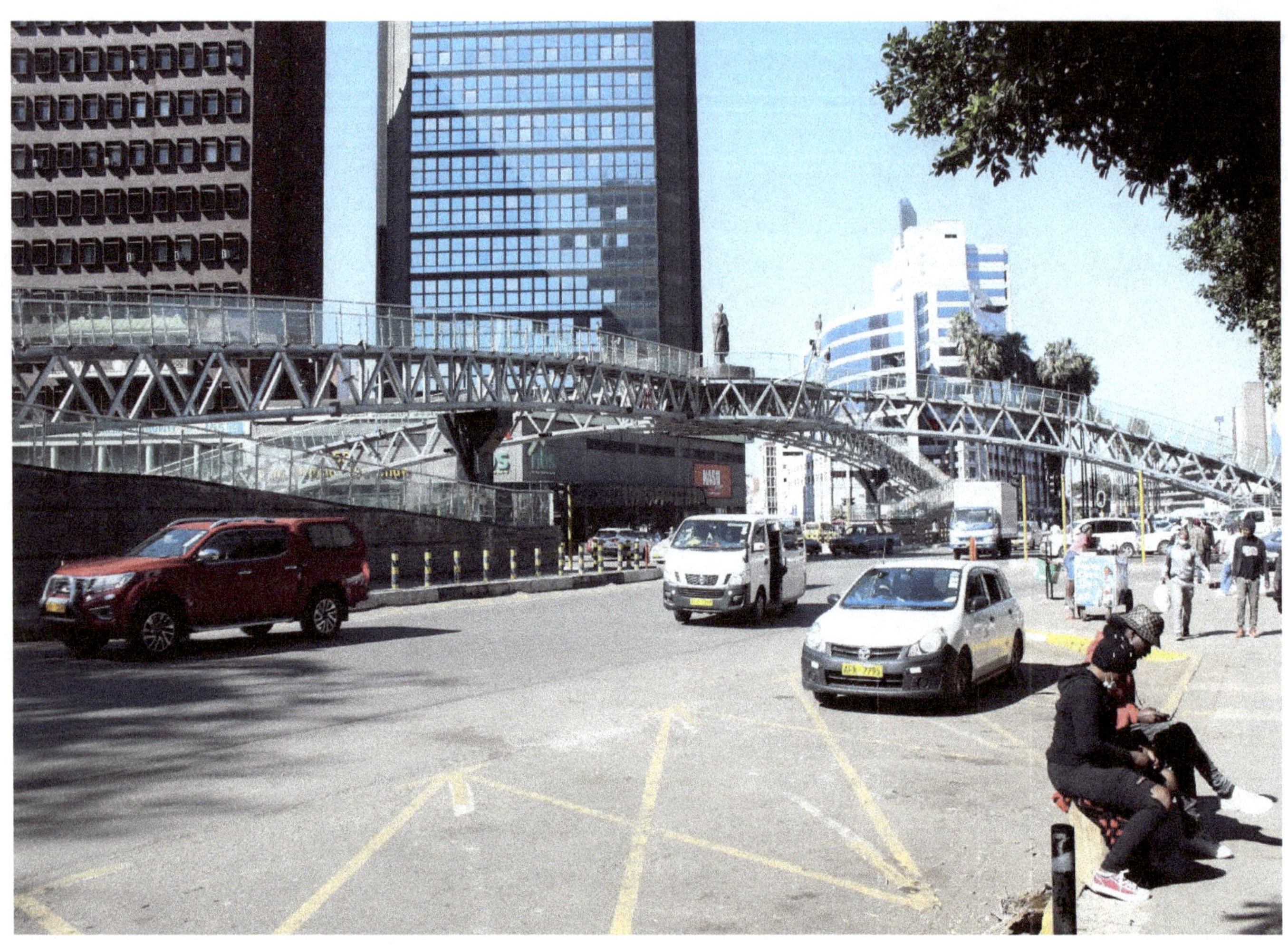

A slice of Harare II,
Digital photography
August 2022

Dear Adonai

Dear Adonai,
Life is ephemeral fashions.
Love is Noise.
Death is Adonai.
Adonai is Death.

We only love their corpses.
We are not pioneers,
we are all after-theory.
The dust is the theory.

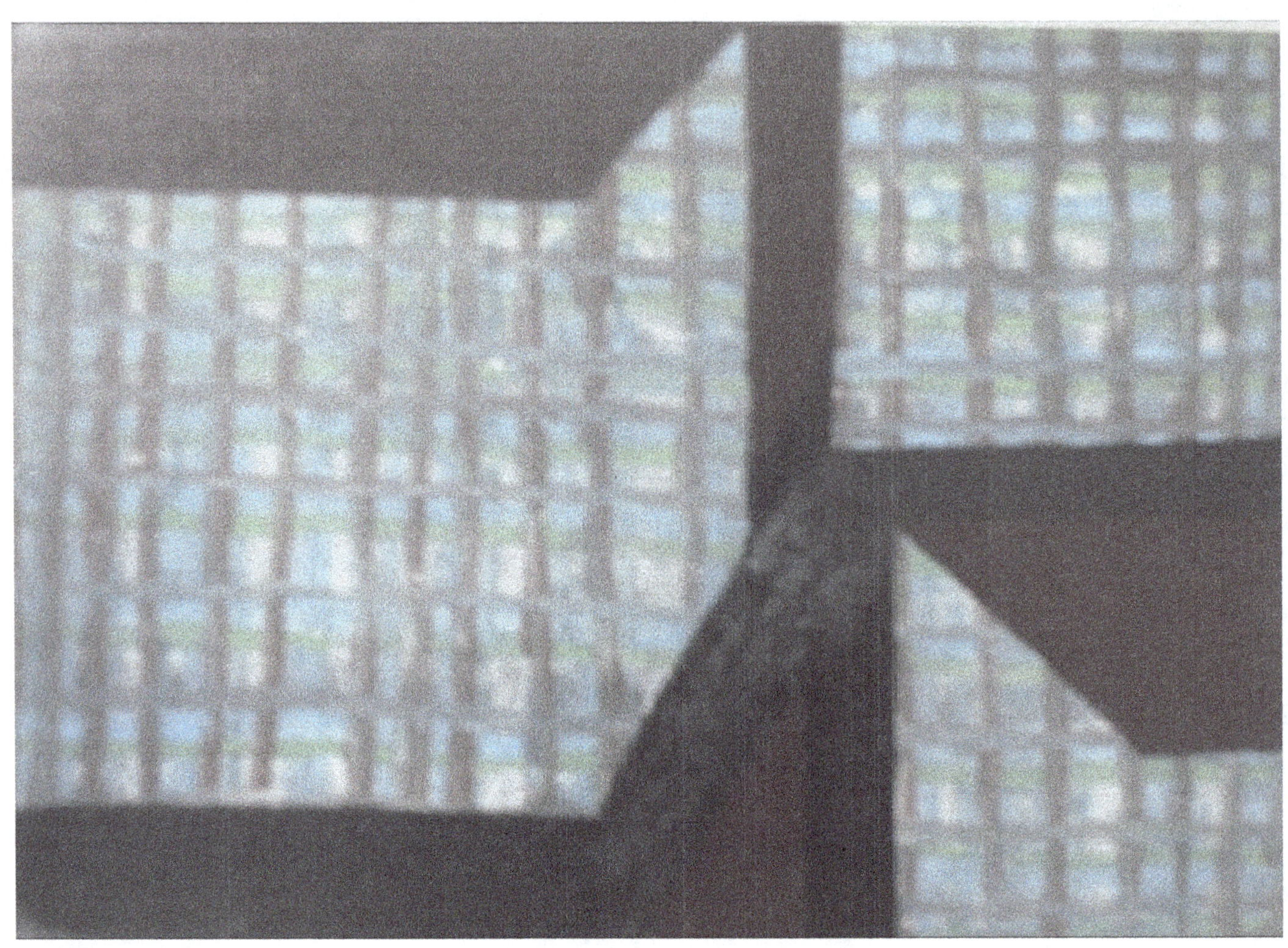

Hongkonging it
Watercolours, acrylics on canvass
Size: 45.7cm by 60.9cm
Year 2022

To Believe in Ghosts

To believe in ghosts is to touch things that cannot be seen. To believe in ghosts is to believe that at that point of death what they were attempting to do is what they will continue doing. If she was coming to see you, know that the next knock you seem to hear at the doors, or windows, or roof is her coming to see you. But you won't notice the night had arrived, waiting to strangle you from behind. To believe in ghosts is to believe the absence she left in your life should be equal to her presence now as a ghost in your life as you hunger from loss remembered. As she beholds everything that is not yours, and everything that is hers, you always thought she would look like, you know, the past, believing in reclamation. To believe in ghosts is to believe that if you kill yourself, death would know you are in love with her.

To believe in ghosts we shouldn't think haunting is ours alone, as everything that lives and dies haunts. To believe in ghosts is to believe your obsession with beef, chicken, or pig's meat has a beginning, you are haunted.

Please Stop This!
Sorry, the Artist's intention is not to make you a herbivore. It's just trajectory and suspension hanging between the doorways of narrative and footnote, human or divine.

To believe in ghosts is to believe animals have souls too, but suppose you say they don't have souls, imagine the rage they would have. They have nothing to fill the empty space between spirit and heaven. Humans do that with happiness.

Ikoko ikoko kunoshamisa ikoko, kudenga, kusisisina mitoro, mitoro inorema, shungu dzorira nengorozi dzotenderera kunoshamisa ikoko (There, there, it's a wonder, there, the heavens, no burdens, the burdens that weighs us down, the dreams mourning, and angels circle around it, it's a wonder, there.)
This is how humans use spirit and heaven to absolve themselves from blame!
To believe in ghosts is to know that language!

To believe in ghosts is to pray for strong cages that can bind their rage inside.

PPS: Okay, I revise my position.

Maybe the artist is trying to make you see the patient contradiction in this poem, the way the word "wound" can mean injury, but as well mean something that's built into something. That animals could have died because of hunger doesn't hold here, believe me, there is no difference between hunger and anger, and there is no small anger

To believe in ghosts is to now think of your mind always digging graves, hunkering to live underground. To believe in ghosts is to realize how funny it is that we fail to give ghosts flesh but allow them to have memory, a memory that resides in dried bones and flesh, and thus building something between cathedral and catacombs.

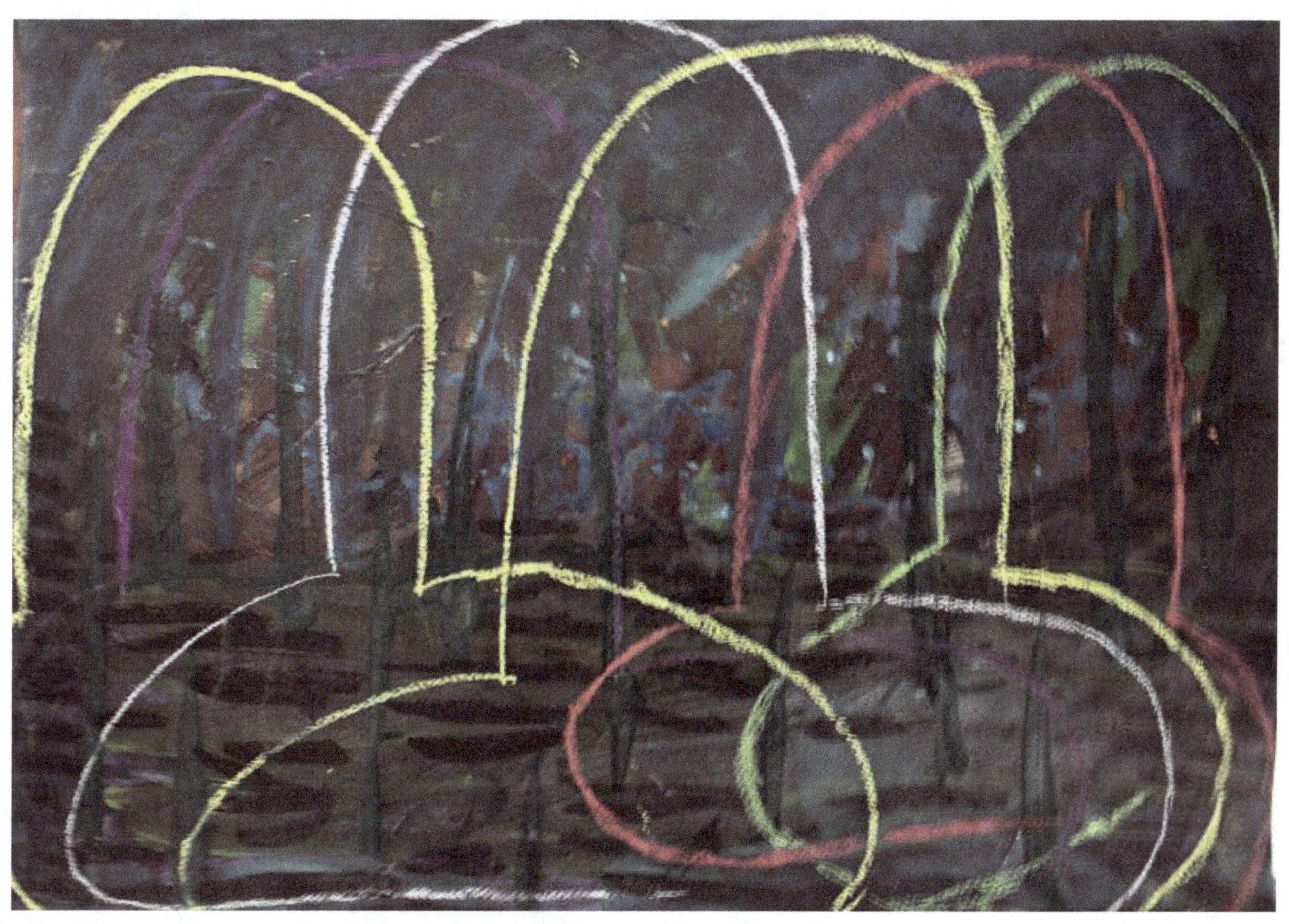

Connections II
Medium: acrylics, watercolours, and pastels on fabriano paper
Year: 2022

Love of Broken Things

In love with all things broken, I am lost in the glimmering reverie of entering, leaving them and unleaving them. In and out, in and out, in and out, I never really leave them to malinger over empty fields, where I am not there.
Loving broken things has been my full time occupation!
It's even weird enough now that I can inhabit my own skin to recount these scars, lost etymologies and lousy jobs of loving broken things.

My love as a kind of unbuilding, our little concessions, our little decisions, our little movements, our little situations and then another day I pull out the harsh out of our quarrels, It's time to swim to the singing gods.

The walking away is never enough, okay there are some horizons I would go that are probably longer than usual, the wide ways around stations, the way you might need to floor the gas pedal to eat up the miles.

To believe that I am in love with her, that I am her boyfriend, and her to keep shoring up that belief in sympathy and exploitation. To keep seeing her for her soft vessel, my taste buds and our earths.

Dear love, love is love is the playing ground between the masculine god Ghede of life and death and the feminine god Erzulie of love, the tangling and meshing of winged forks exploding off in Haiti.

Lost is my official status

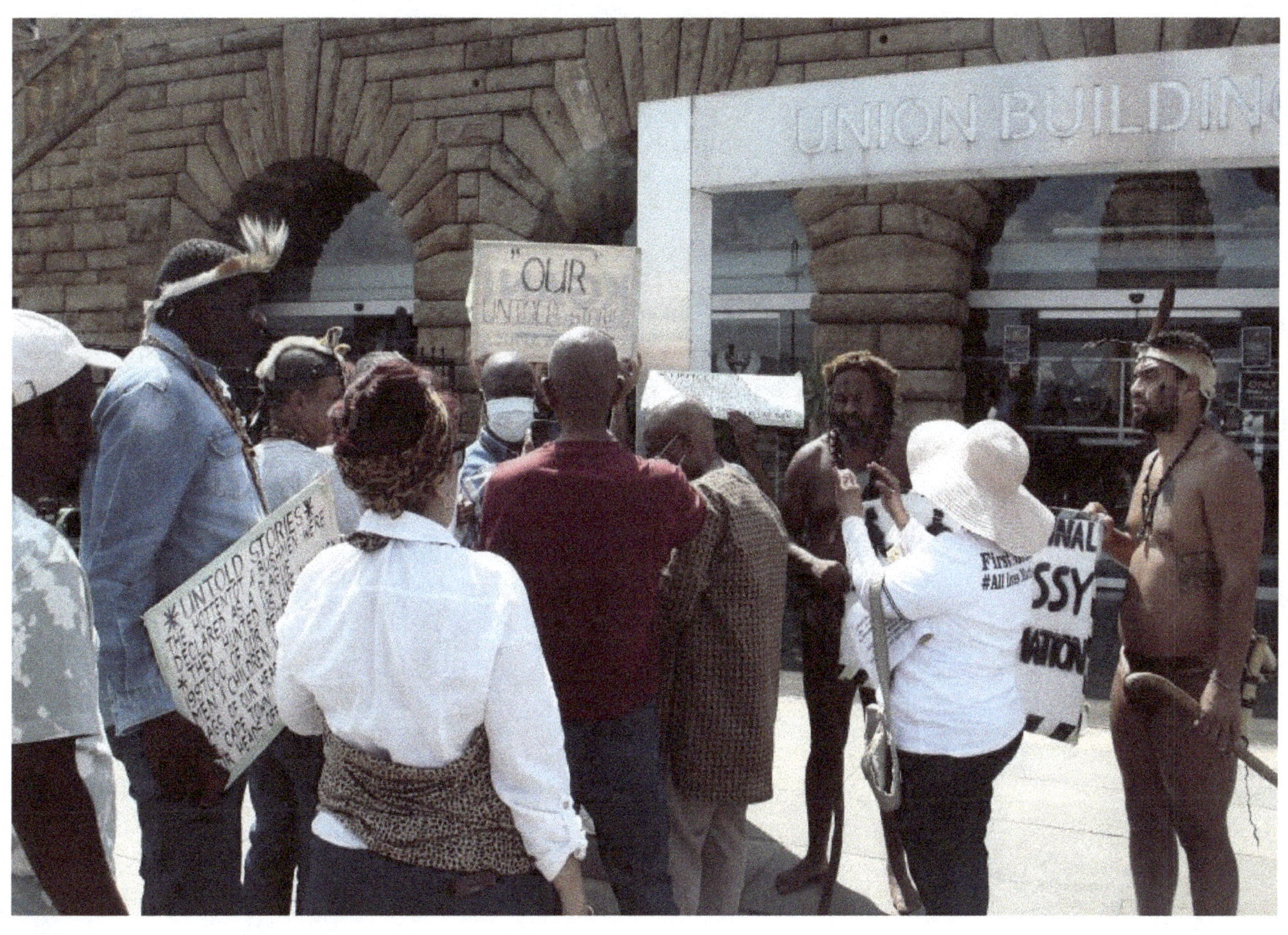

Khoisan people standing up to authority,
Digital photography
March 2022, Pretoria, South Africa

Use a Spoon

The spoon on the table with bread and a cup of tea. The spoon and a bowl of rice, a spoon full of honey lapping your tongue. The spoon on your palm emptying sugar. The spoon and macaroni and cheese. The spoon as a wedge. The spooning that is for the bed.

The spoon in a glass, stirring, and the hands holding the glass and spoon. The spoon to measure dusty chemicals. The spoon as key. The spoon of water emptying out the oceans.

The spoon as a shovel imitating the spoon. The spoon as an opposite of the knife. The spoon to transient factories pouring out pallet stacks and snack bars. The spoons scrapping, scratching, cutting, capping…true life is housewives.

The spoon as a surgical instrument. To suffocate yourself with a spoon

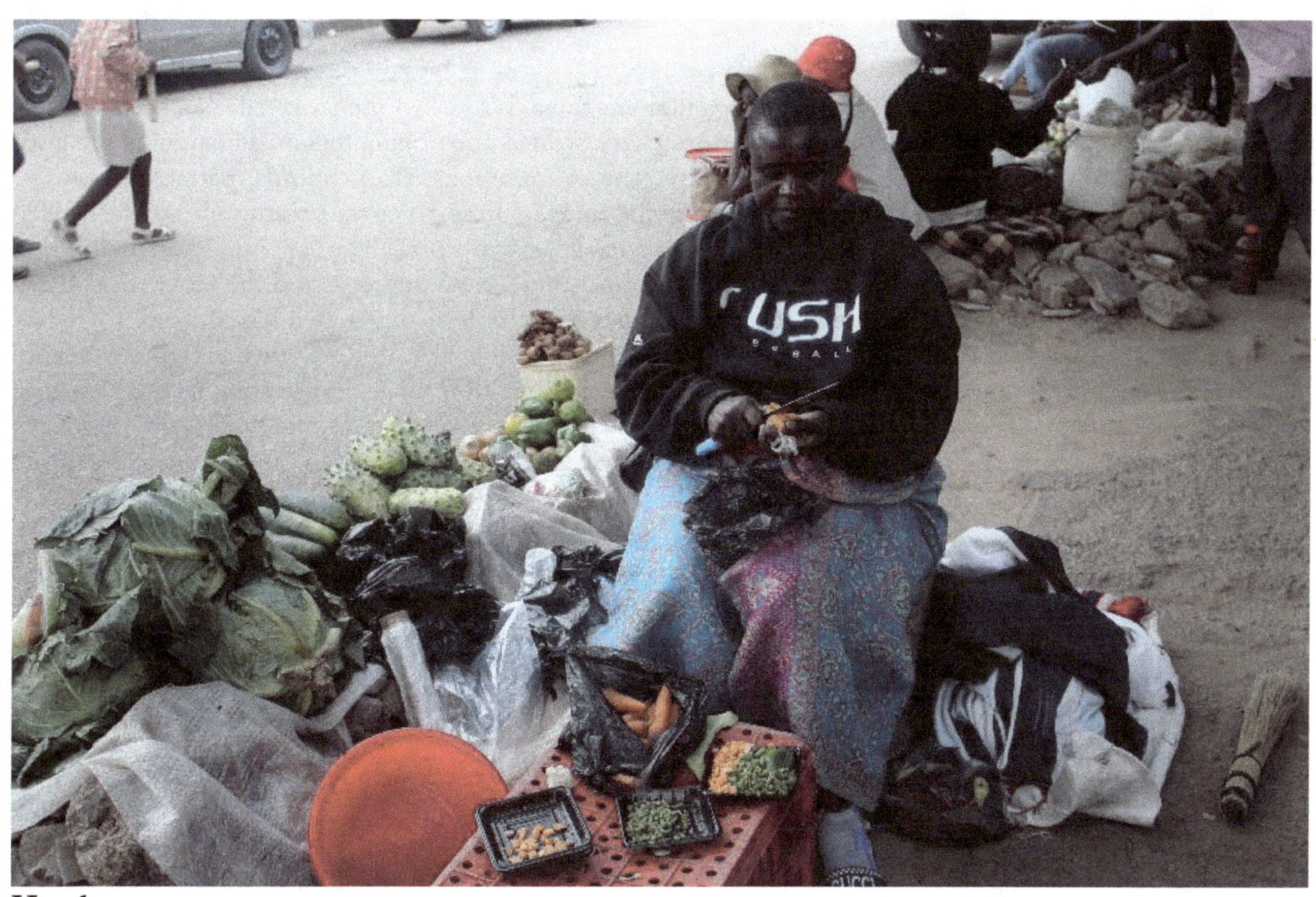

Hustle,
Digital photography
Chitungwiza, Zimbabwe, June 2022

The poet is the god

Vertical are the axis lines to the universes and horizontal are the axis lines to the storyteller's stories. At the perpendicular intersection of the universe and the storyteller's stories, the poet enters in. The poet is the god. The god dances in ritual, languages, metaphors, drums, flutes, marimbas, story-strands, patterns, diseases, possessions and haunted feelings of trapped souls lost in the rings of time, to cover up emptiness. The artists' body should always support the poem like illness speaking itself as symptoms. The raw hug of living several lifetimes, I am here, I was there; I went from there to here to hear. Where universe and the story meet there is formlessness, and art is what language fails to state. In Chinese mythology that which has ultimate form has no form. It should move for the gods move, moving creates possible forms through maintaining beauty throughout movement. To translate a buried memory, haunts, orientation from fissure song to fissure song, from wound song to wound song, to build a mighty trauma from the missing pieces, the poet is the doorways to the spirit, a hewn off the skin. The poet is an Adam still beholden to the earth!

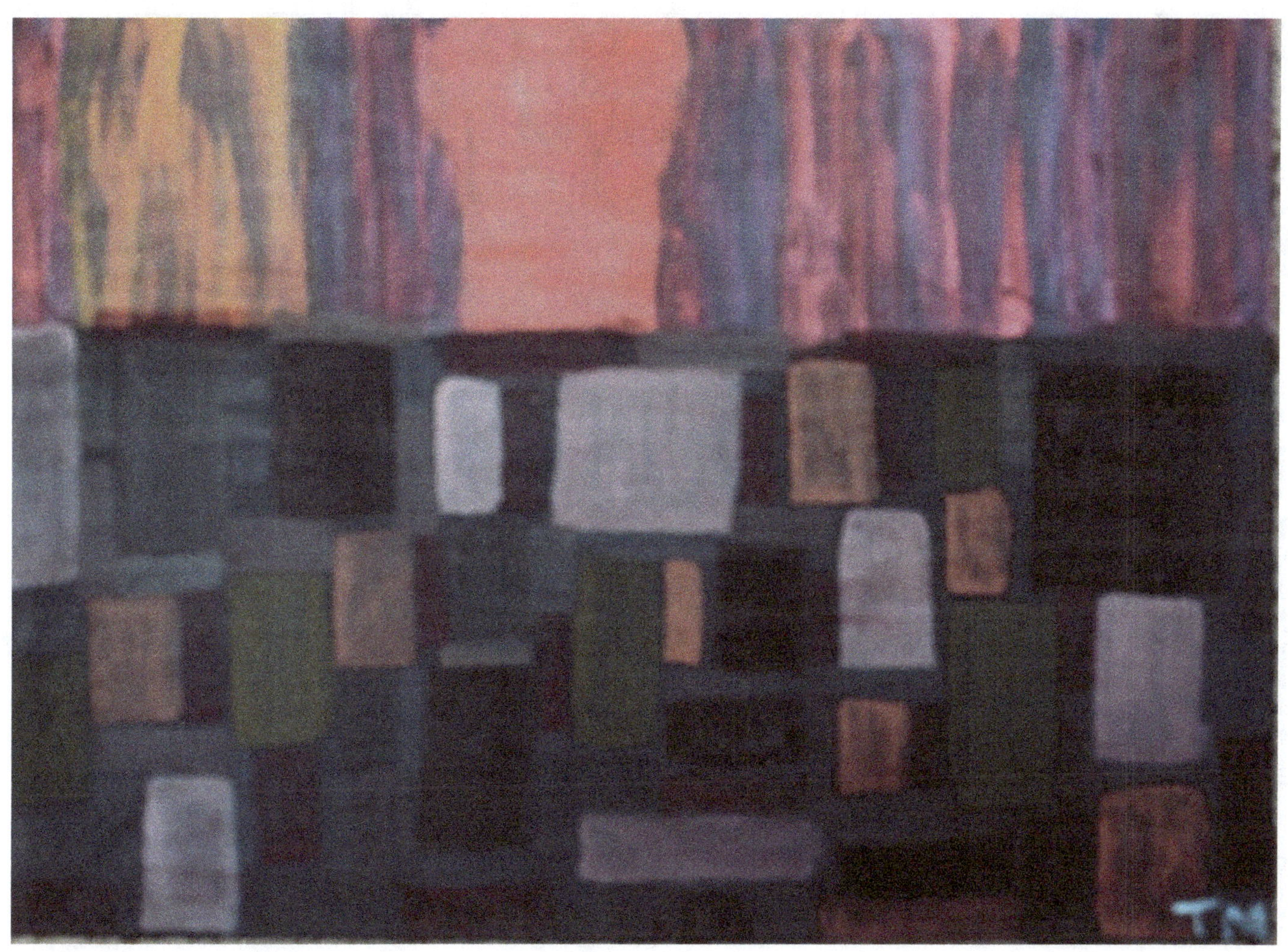

Keeping the red sun away
Watercolours and acrylics on canvass
Size: 45.7cm by 60.9cm
Year 2022

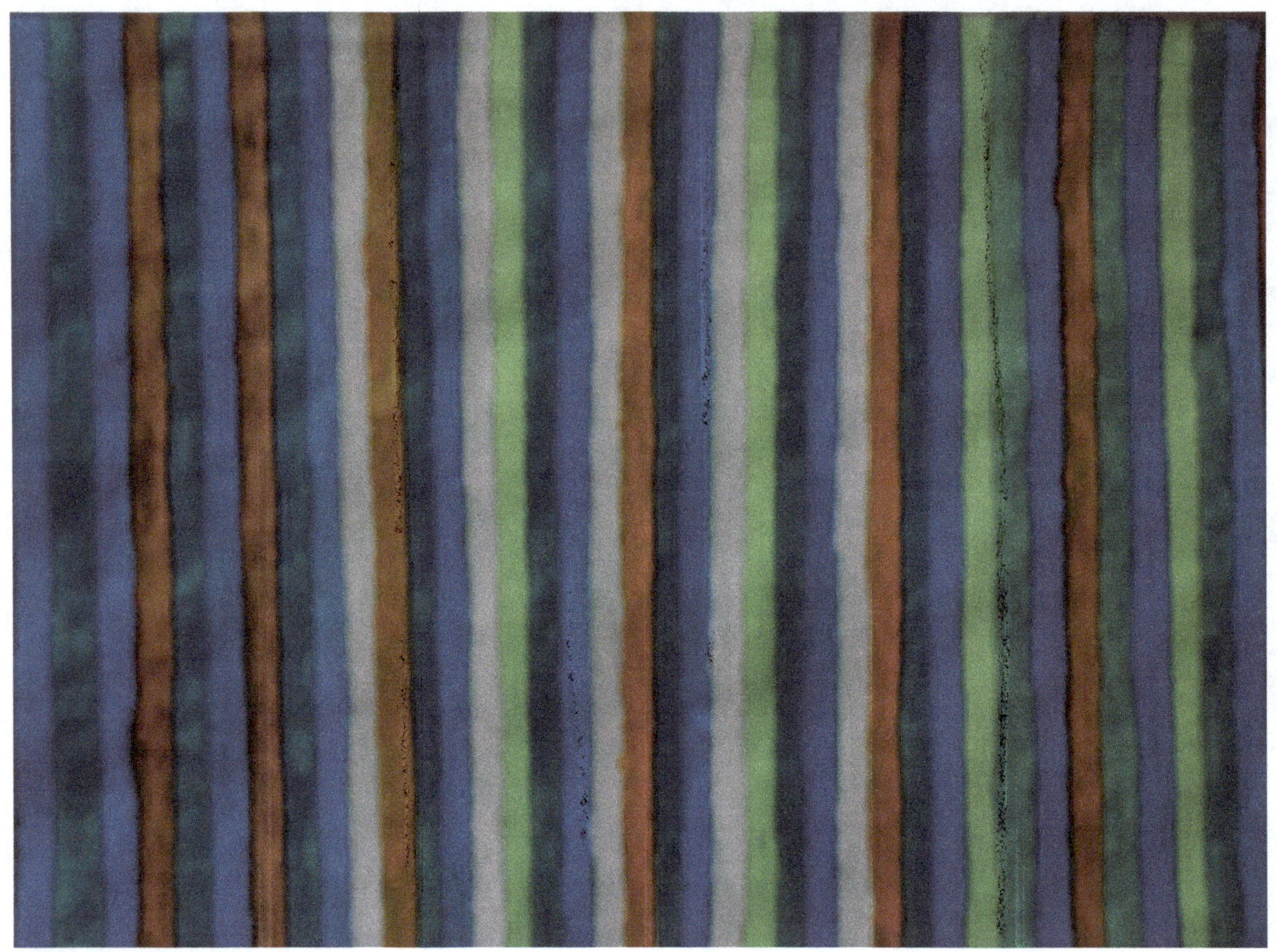

Lines
Watercolours and acrylics on fabriano paper
Size 29.7cm by 42cm
Year: 2022

The Lines We Pray To

The ivory grey lines that changes yearly the soils of your face
The smoky lines that disappears by being visible
The liminal lines that look lifelike the more things look alike
The lines that are old maps without legs
The lines that allows us to imagine a life different from ours now
The lines that matches each map to its corresponding referent
The laughing blood lines exploding where the sun lies shedding its golden skins in the west
The crackling lines that will bring down a house with laughter
The lines in the conversations of the dove birds at night's fall
The lines that make humming birds turn around to see the source of their songs
The dark lines that becomes light, the light that becomes dark lines
The day's lines that can be left to a day at the end of the day
The lines of evening's corroborator announcing what spoils are there to deplete
The lines that screams into ears of dark nights for light to appear
The lines that make people meet again after separating
The lines that convert hatred into the curiosity of love
The lines that finds the elder sister in the youngest sister
The lines that are boundaries between our bodies
The lines that commemorate what we do not know of each other
The lines that connect songs that cannot be separated
The lines that arose from news of death
The lines that abandons your body before dark bears witness to your being
The lines that hears the sun at night
The lines that punches into the indifferent skies
The lines that distrusts superstitions by believing in myths
The lines that teaches us how to sooth an idea thrown at us as sighs and grunts
The lines that warns everyone of cracks in the road
The lines that studies the river's waves until the river is blind
The lines that walks the line and still find the river

The lines that keep despair at bay and assuage it with longing
The lines that shows you no one is coming

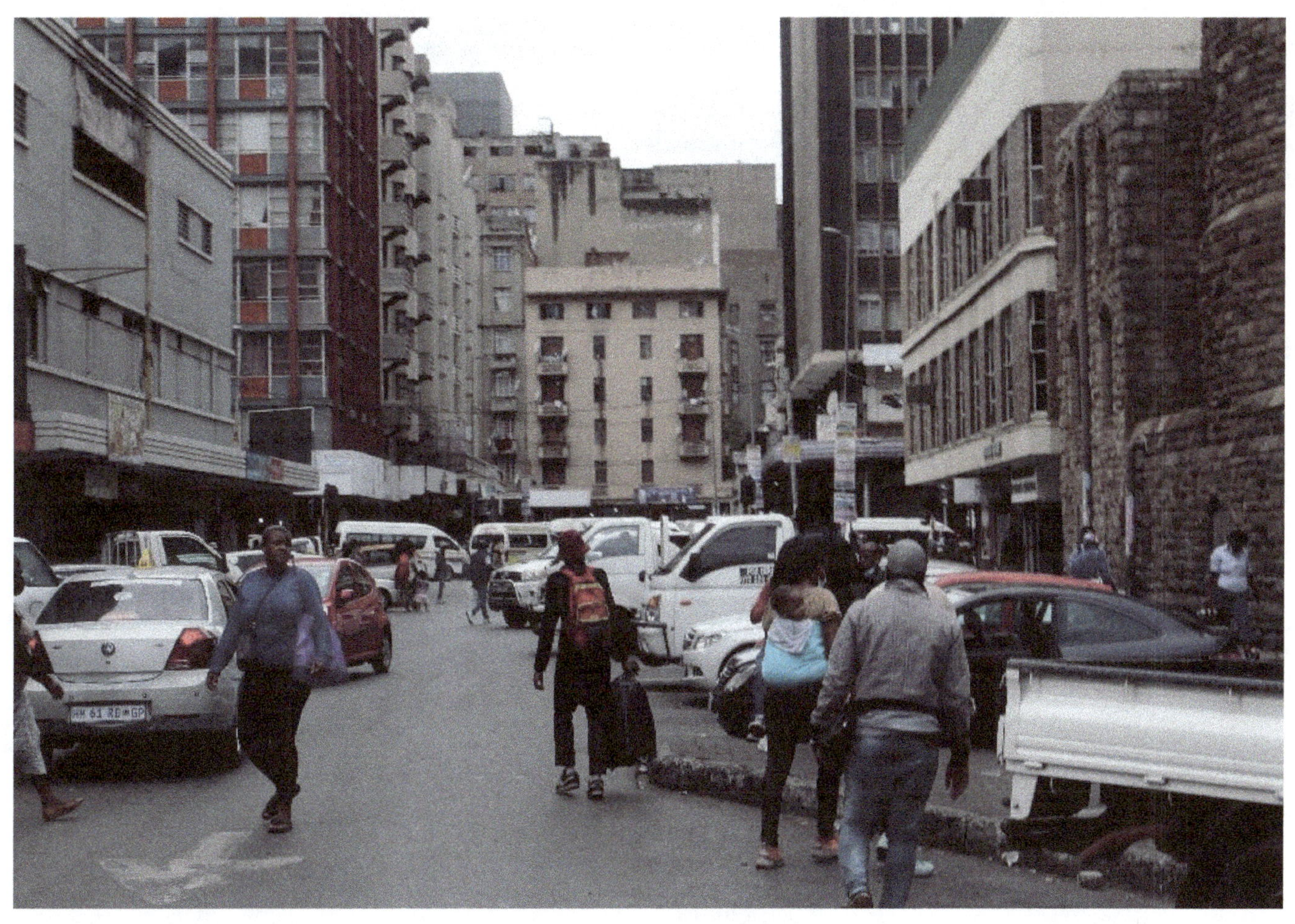

The streets of Johannesburg,
Digital photography
South Africa, February 2022

Standing below an argument

I am standing below an argument, resetting its thinking fangs in the movements above my head. It wets me, as it trickles down my head. I try to wipe it off with my hands, I try to probe the skies to staunch off its pores, something blood and haunt stays on my hands. It whispers, this is the only place for you outside the nut house, and you don't even have enough insanity. Home is what you have left behind.

An argument once open, is always a little open, you feel it, but you cannot move in tandem with it.

Memory is now your constant companion, you are never alone, but some days mourn your friends.

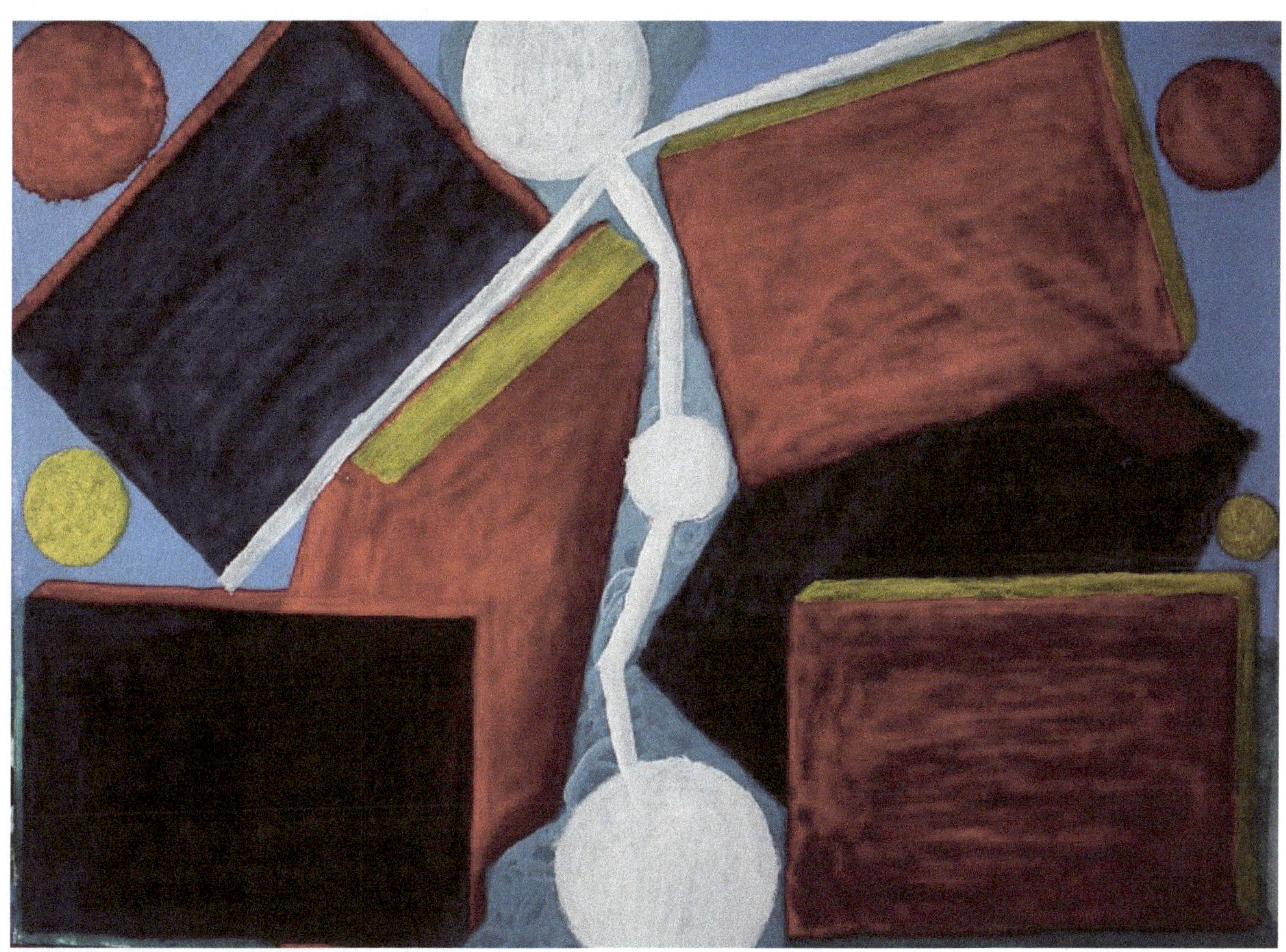

Meditation series #4
Acrylics on canvass
Size: 42cm by 59.4cm
Year: 2022

Meditation series #4

The black and red books that immerse their weight on a constricted shrinking human form, who is three white circles joined together by thick white lines. The circles represent the head, the middle and the lower part of a human being; the mind, the heart and the sex organs/legs…and a whitish blood can be seen sipping out of the human form. Two red circles (representing the conscious, the sun, the light…) and two yellow circles (representing the unconsciousness, the moon, the darkness…) are the worlds that this human inhabits, that also controls him. What inspired me to use the books and why I allude to the books' damaging the human, comes from my strong doubts on the importance of the black book and other religions' red books to make the human condition better and livable as these books have been used or are being used to jail humans in fear.

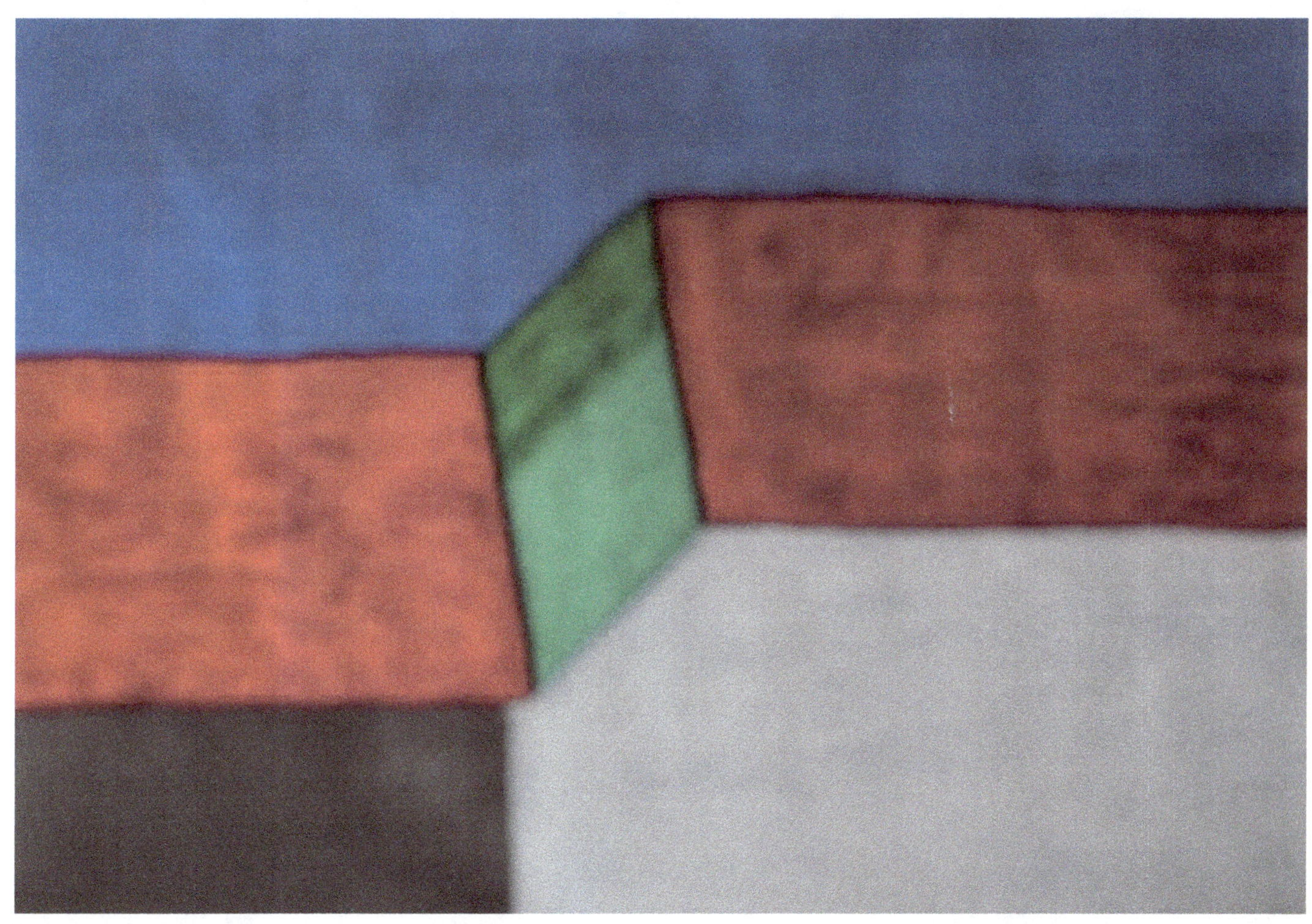

Shape shift
Watercolours and acrylics on fabriano paper
Size: 42cm by 59.4cm
2022

Black is black

Black is black is grey
as naming is cursing is white
as being blessed yellow is not to have a name.

Negro, please!
Let me be your heroin hero on.
Let us learn to try harder

Its people that surround you..., always,
There are people somewhere.

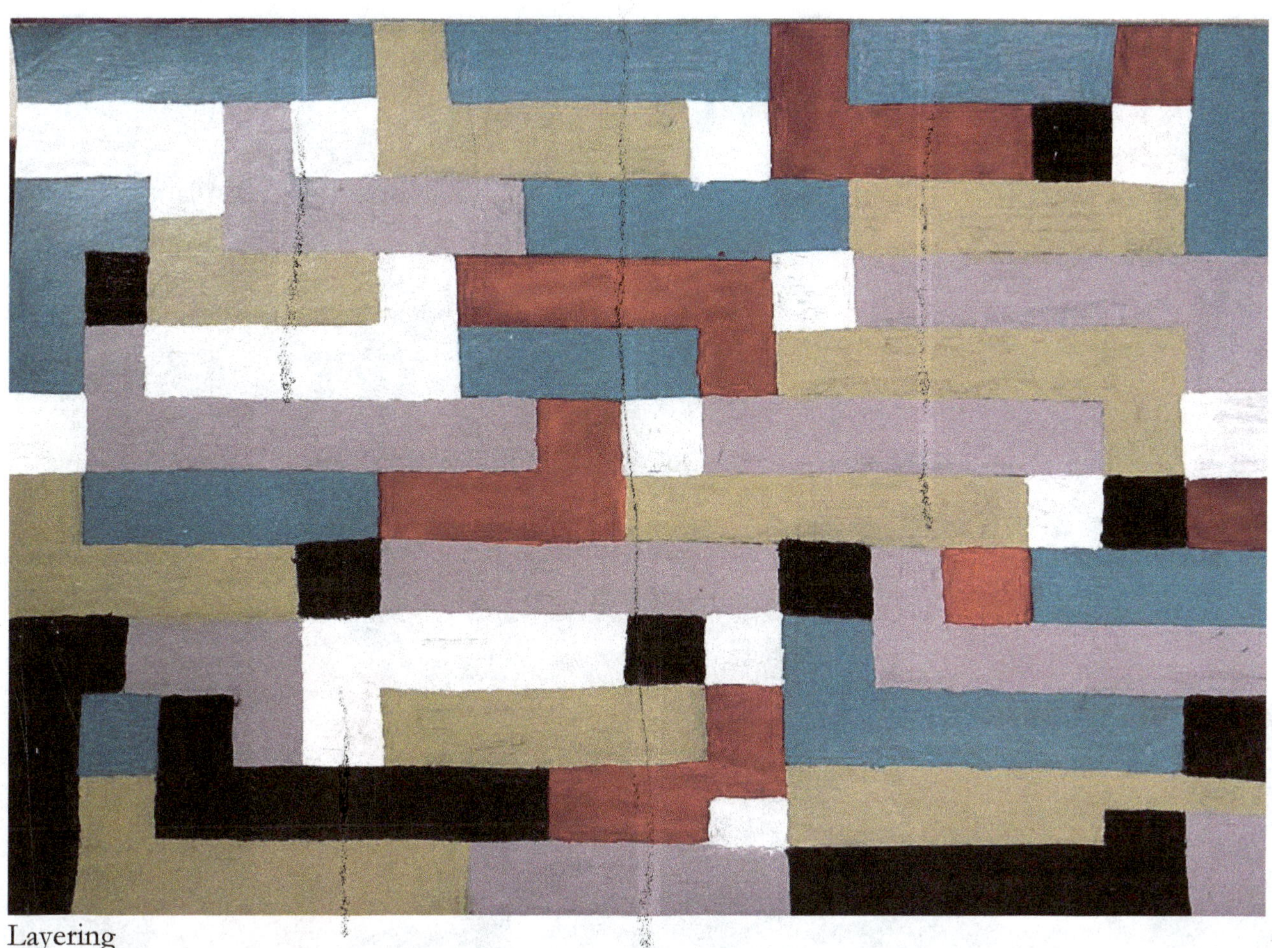

Layering
Acrylics and watercolours on paper
Size: 42cm by 59.4cm
2023

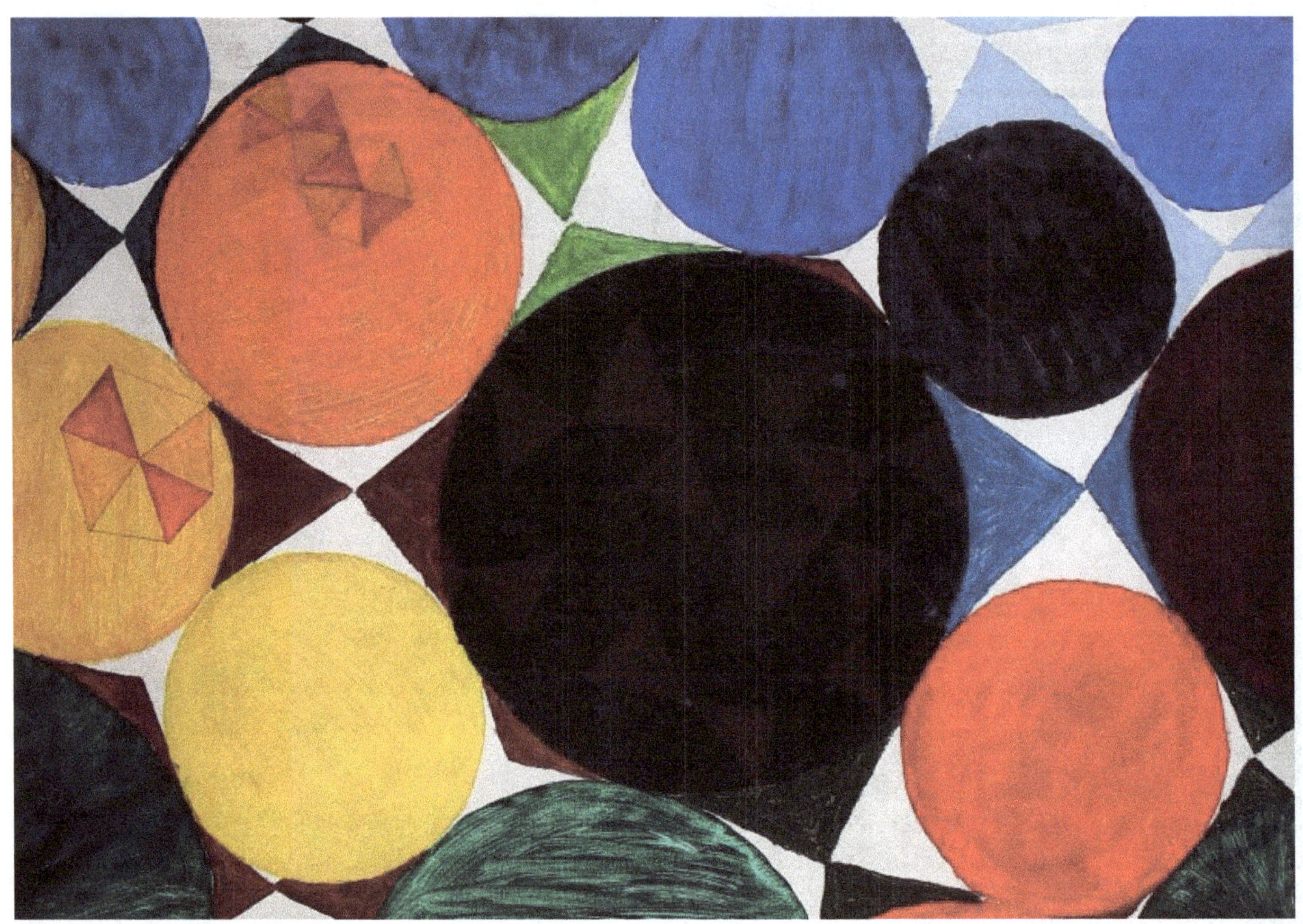

Meditation series #3
Acrylics on canvass
Size: 42cm by 59.4cm
Year: 2022

Meditation series #3

When I started painting this piece I started with the big black circle or ball…and other circles started shaping of it. I want to take the black circle as Africa, black people, darkness. Modern humans, even ancient humans, it is agreed, originated from Africa and blackness has always been associated with the continent…, the black continent, the Dark Continent. Joseph Conrad's Heart of Darkness. And as the colours arrange and move off the black colour they become lighter. Even when we just look at colours, generally speaking there is no colour beyond the other side of black…I mean darker, or blacker than black. Black of the first colour. It is the beginning or beginning of end of colours. Black starts the colours, and all the other colours happen as we tinker with the black colour, by adding a little bit of light and colour to black, thus it creates greys, the browns, reds, greens, yellows etc... What is the light? White is the light, black is darkness…even in the racists' sense black is always associated with darkness and white is associated with light, or more light. It is the white colours in my drawing that holds those interlinking strands. Am I wrestling with racists' thoughts on colours, yes I am, to certain extent. Isn't the white colour always naming the other colours, instead of the black colour doing that as it is the origin of colours and humans. After all its humans who discovered these colours. But the white colour names the other colours, 'you are black, you are yellow, you are brown, you are beige, you are people of colour…' Even when the space occupied by the white colours are small the white colour still has the power to push, to pull the strands off the ground, to create a sense of uprootedness. I need not emphasise how the white race uprooted and disturbed or are still disturbing all the other colours the world over. The geometric triangular shapes that predominates the black colours borrows from genetic coding diagrams, which is a field that is shaping our origin stories.

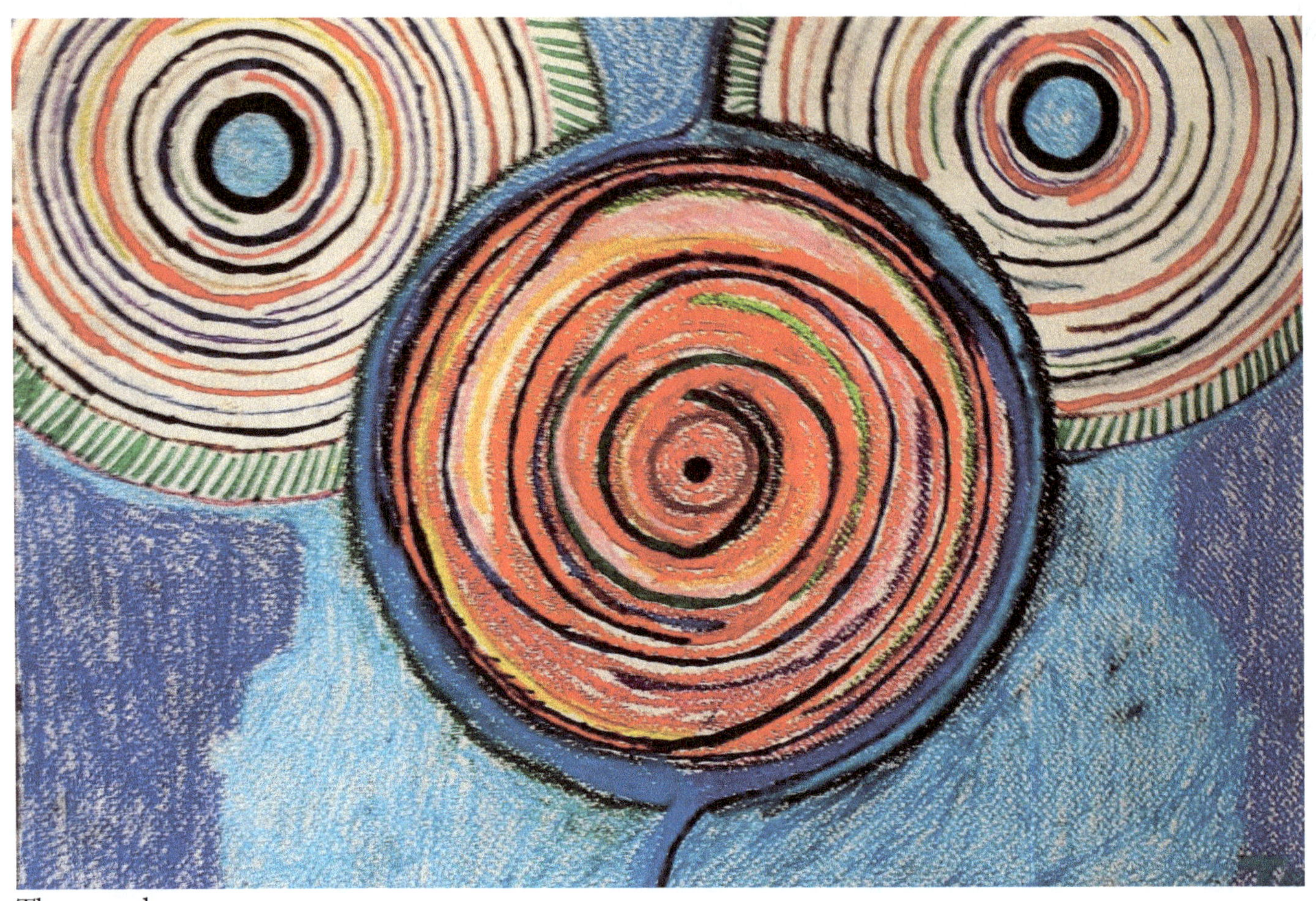

Three eyed
Felt pens, tip pens, markers, oil pastels on fabriano paper
Size 29.7cm by 42cm
Year: 2022

What country did you mistake for being heard, Zimbabwe?

When you delete the ink my words are written on, do you delete the words too. Aren't they still there, written in the mind, wind…? What of the difference between the words that come out of your mouth and the words that stays in my mind. What were those words before you think them, say them- did I write them? Where do your words go after you say them? Whose words were they if I had repeated their stories every time someone asked me to tell stories? Us standing in the landlady's yard at the cottage I rented, my mouth running away with their bag of stories, about a molecular homecoming. You can see for yourself I like it when I am the one doing the misunderstanding, bent into the questioning and listening. What shall you make of this leveling out of meaning, you explaining about words that want to be of sound and sight? What do you make of words that look and see where there is nothing outlined. What do you think of the words like a dumb rock cartographer's eye that cannot draw the map of grief, the words like dead women waking up in my stories, in yours? Of the words we wield so nicely like bending into the intent that was never meant to be. What of words the door that opens and closes your mind against language. Words that protect you from guilty wars you wage upon waking. What do you make of words you have uttered as a constant ritual of looking at yourself carefully as you grow older and bitter? What country did you mistake for being heard, Zimbabwe? What sounds human at that level? Sorry fellow, let me let you let me breath. Let impulse be the theory, and I will just let this be an oblation to words- but I would rather my lines were Zimbabwean lines!

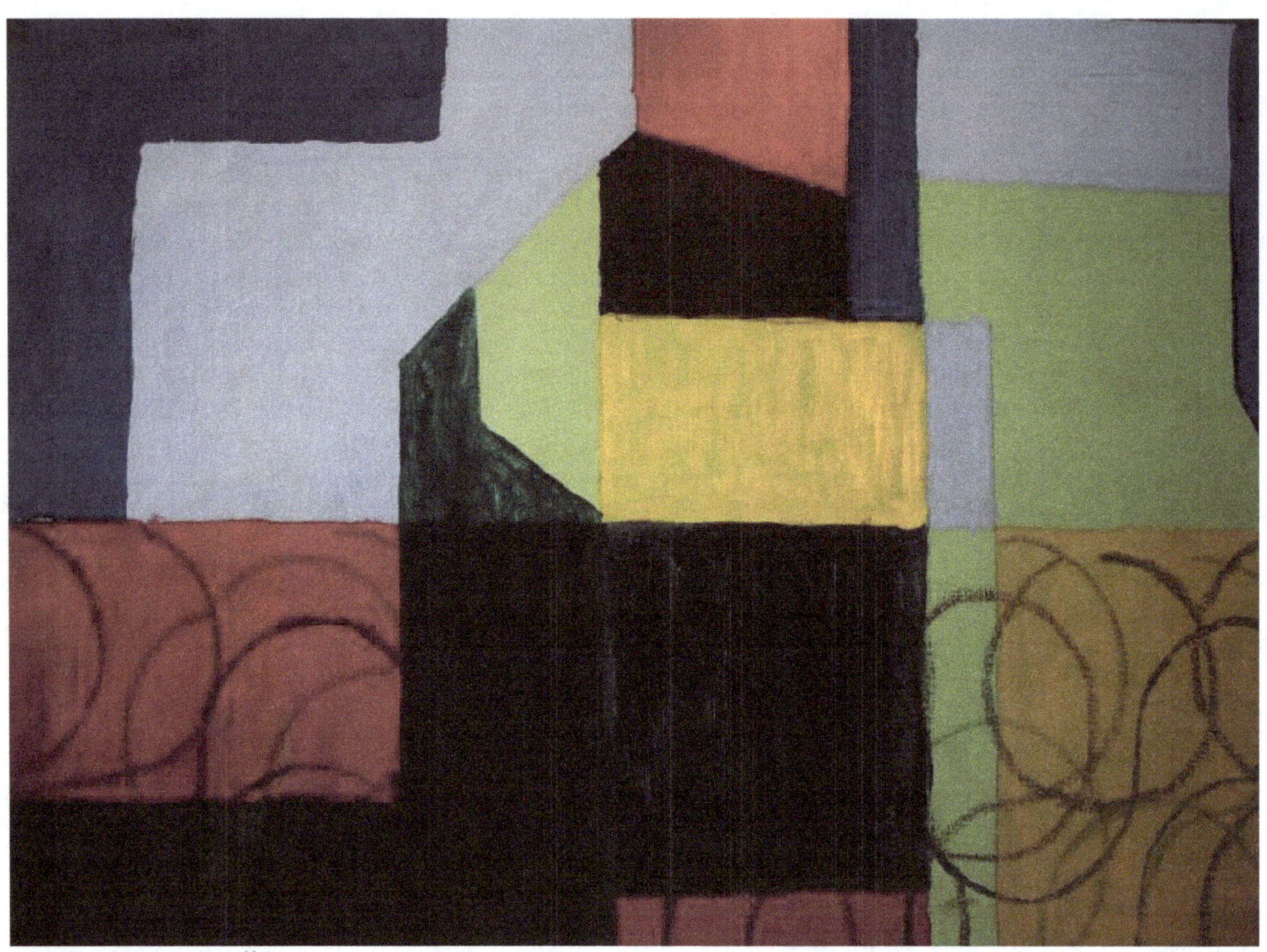

Meditation series #5
Acrylics on canvass
Size: 42cm by 59.4cm
Year: 2022

Meditation series #5

The obsession, which I have maintained for years with circles, boxes, lines, and blocks continues. The way things merge, immerse and emerge into each other, some disappearing below the surface, to resurface further. The concentric circles dulls, strengthens, and disappears, only to reappear as the colours change. This drawing uses the architectural lines and shapes to propose a view which is transient and at the same time fixed, like time. Time is a view. Time is perspective. What the eyes see as they move from one narrative to the next narrative ultimately trips the viewer

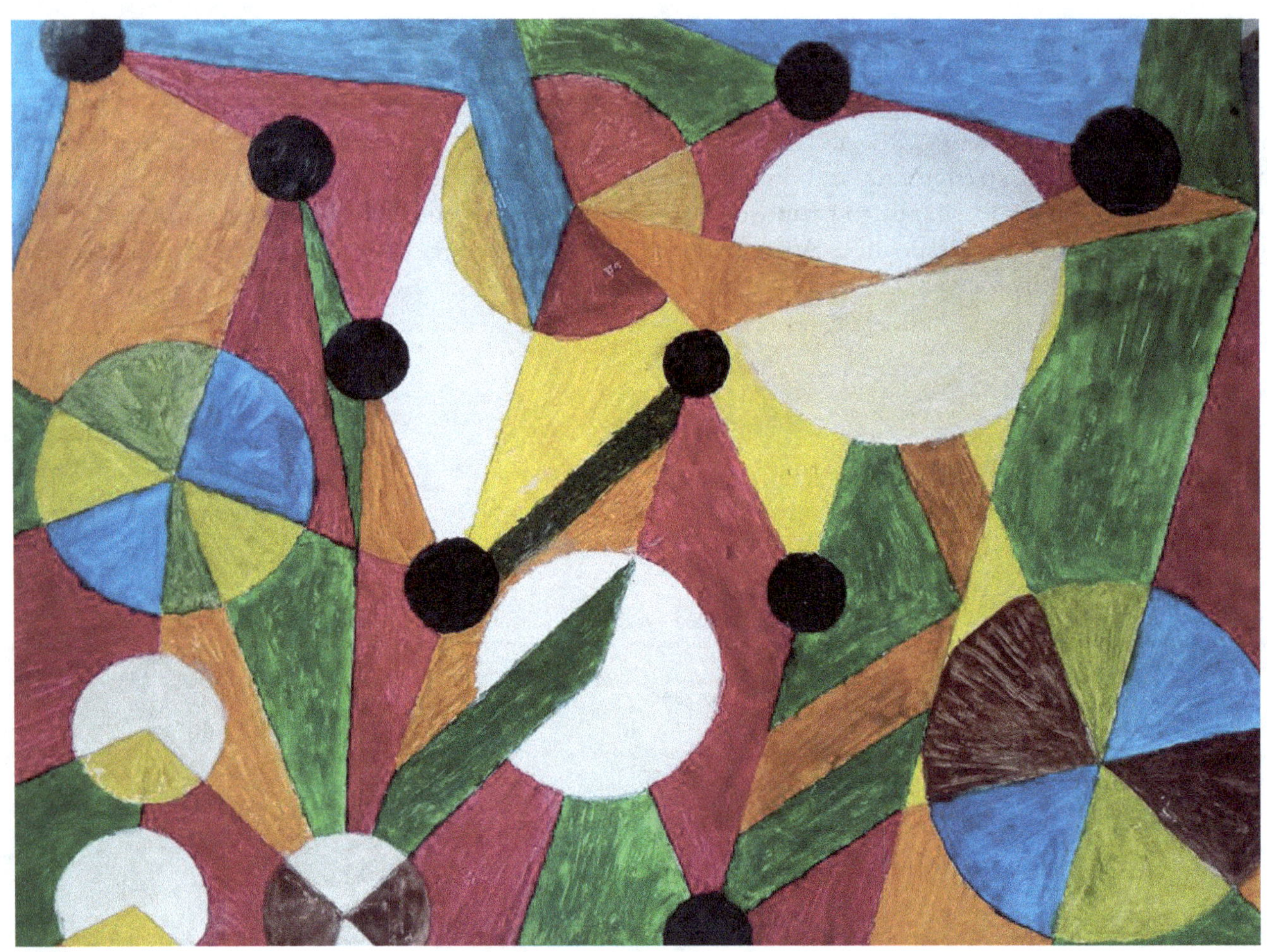

Falling
Acrylics and watercolours on paper
50cm by 65cm
2023

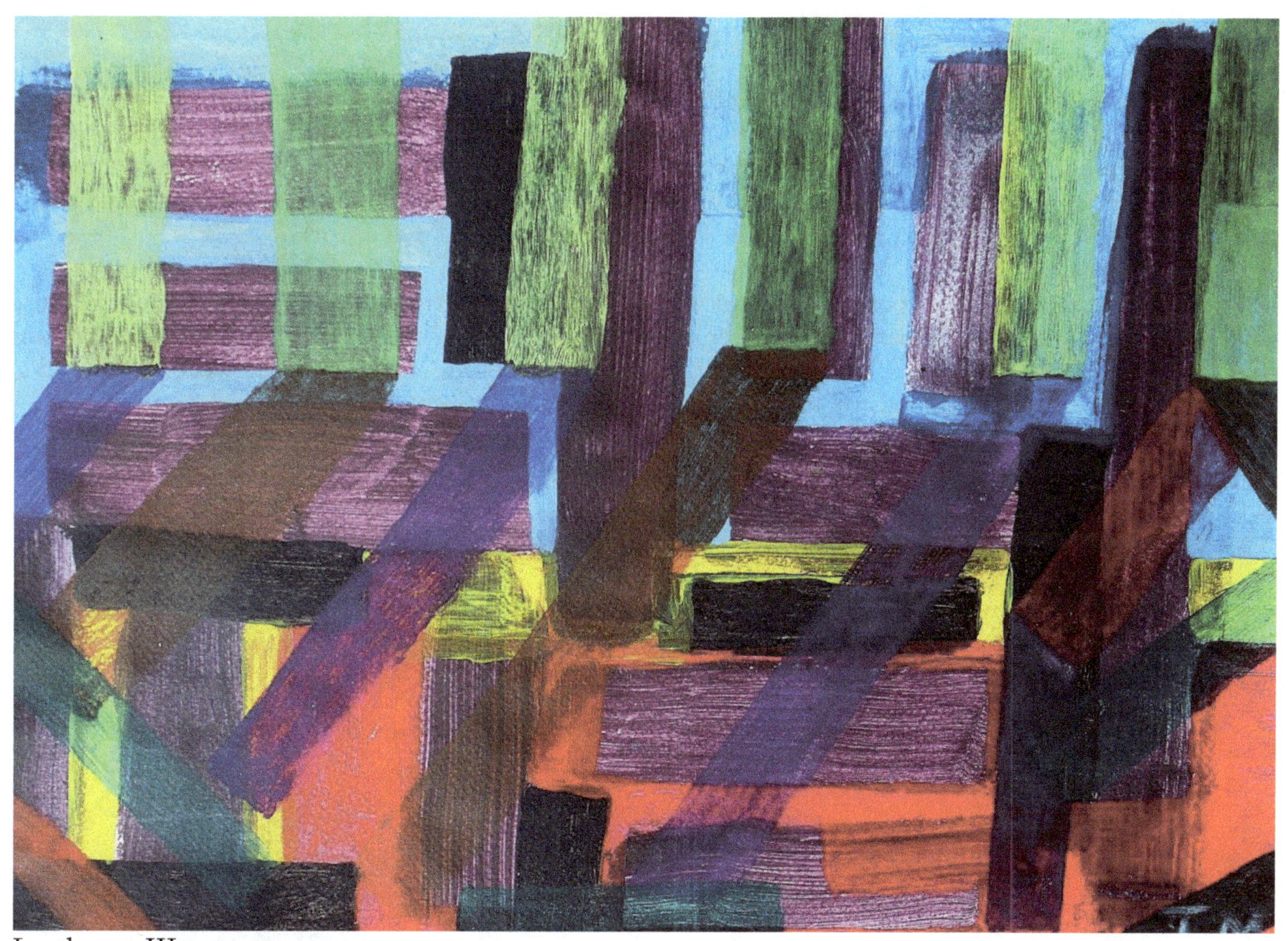

Landscape III
Watercolours and acrylics on fabriano paper
Size 29.7cm by 42cm
Year: 2022

Silence is Gold

Silence was never golden; you could never take it to the bank to add to the zeroes. We were a noisy family, and whoever would shout the loudest knew accompaniment far more than melody. And I was the loudest one. We made noise fighting, laughing, arguing, telling stories… We were loud as we confronted neighbours who stole our goats and ate all the evidence. We were like honeybees exhibiting conscious and unconscious behaviours, our voices tangling and untangling in the wind in altruistic improvement of the stock.

Our father didn't like it, always complained about our noise like the class monitor; booked us, punished us, always trying to tame us, but failed. Like bees remembering where certain flowers were and navigating our own exploding figures, bodies and circles by smell, sun angles, moon distances to the flowers, we created a hive mind, always consumed in constructing beautiful buildings.

Now as the call of the dust is the loudest, the only other sounds are of me and of what cannot be hidden by the rooms I sleep in and the beddings. Always gasping for silence, hot as a major ceremony among the living, I have left nothing on my beddings but my huff; you won't decipher anything about me from it. Read me as read is both present and past tense, as I stare loudly at nothing- silence staring silently at my empty hands. Read me to realize that my books are like me, they are slow to make friends but hard to let go if befriended. Read me to know there is a Nyanga in the lines of my hands, along the tapering fingers, of the villages down there, somewhere in the east.…

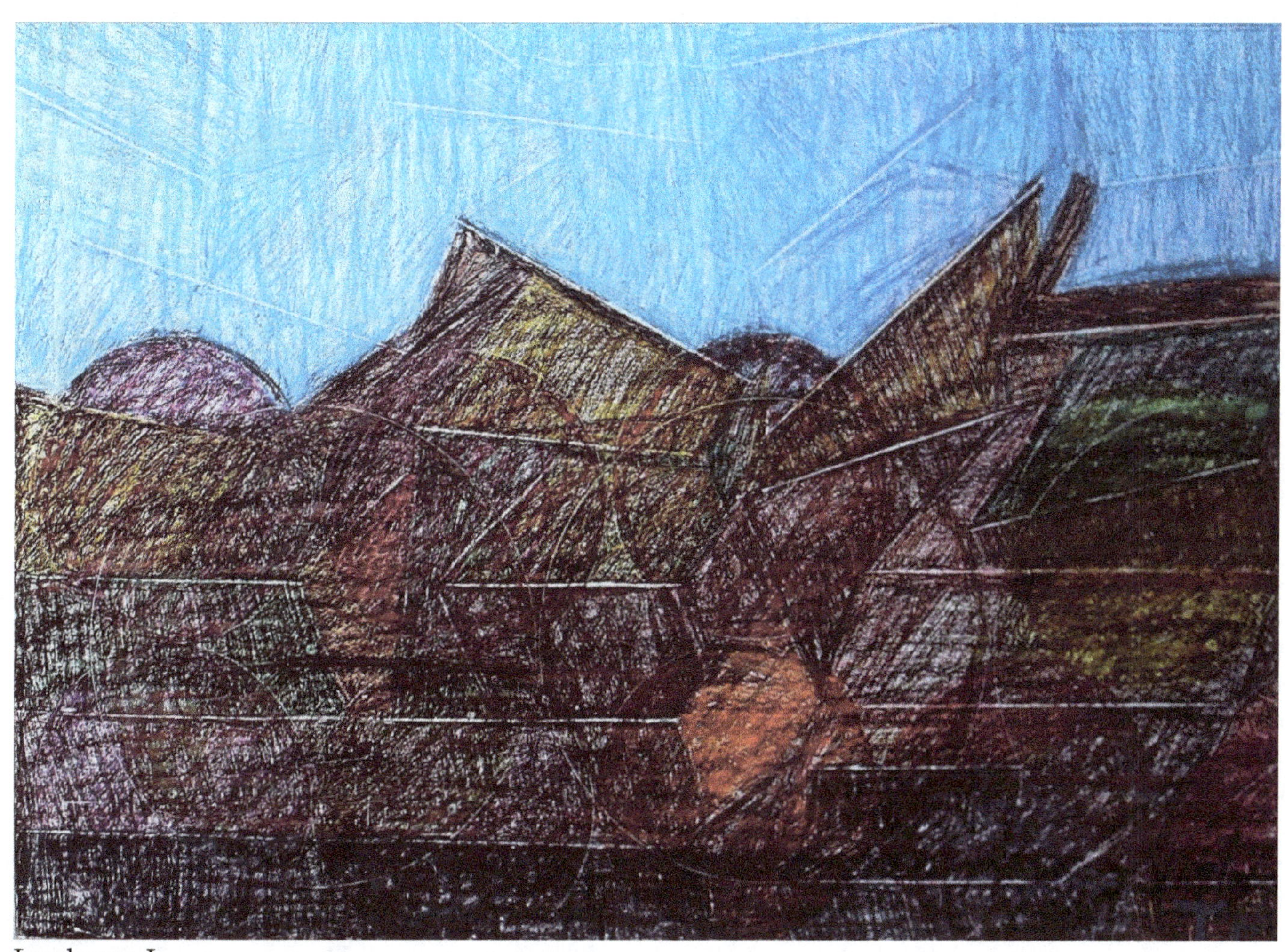

Landscape I
Oil pastels on white board
Size: 42cm by 59.4cm
2022

An unutterable question mark without an answer?

As the faces that stare askance out of our eyes look like death, rainy muddy ivory; like the skins of my grandmother's callused hands- it doesn't matter that it is time when spring bends into summer, when clouds mirror wings of demons, maybe of parents and grandparents who left us on this pieces of stones. It doesn't even matter it's the rain that moves time, no matter where you are now, its rain that told you what time it was, when to go, where the wind was.

How will I explain it to myself that behind this boy's closed eyes laid the browns of a violin returning to silence as the priest recite sonnets instead of last rites? That no one escapes this suffering, that there is no need for praying here, but to just breathe, for even dust finds its way inside closed buildings. That losing you is minuscule against this grief descending, weightlessness, torrential…, coming in two pairs, as broken June's cold winds made of shafts of glass and as soft spoken yellow shafts of November's light.

How will I explain to myself that when they put your body into the ground, my mouth kept moving of its own accord, trying to find words that you aren't here, and that you aren't somewhere else too? Alms of being heard, that there are no spirits to pin this on a new hymn yet to arrive. And at the end, did I say, come down, the ground will rock you as you moved to the centre. Descending into, into, into.., the earth, did I check your face for beautiful noise around your eyes, lips, forehead, shimmering like the last hour.

That the lunar melodies for astronomers are the songs of the frogs for sailors, that Astronomy is both science and mythology, let me not tell you of the mathematics that failed to treat the flu that surrounded you, the myth that decided which of the two ways to go against the ground, and that you can still hear the music of the universe.

Would it have made any difference if we had known the ground is an unutterable question mark without an answer? Is there a signboard of what's buried below where we stand now, a million years ago? There is, is there, such thing as solid ground? Trust me, you have been here before, at that moment you began to suspect it's really your voice.

Would it have made much difference if we had known it was towards the end of you?

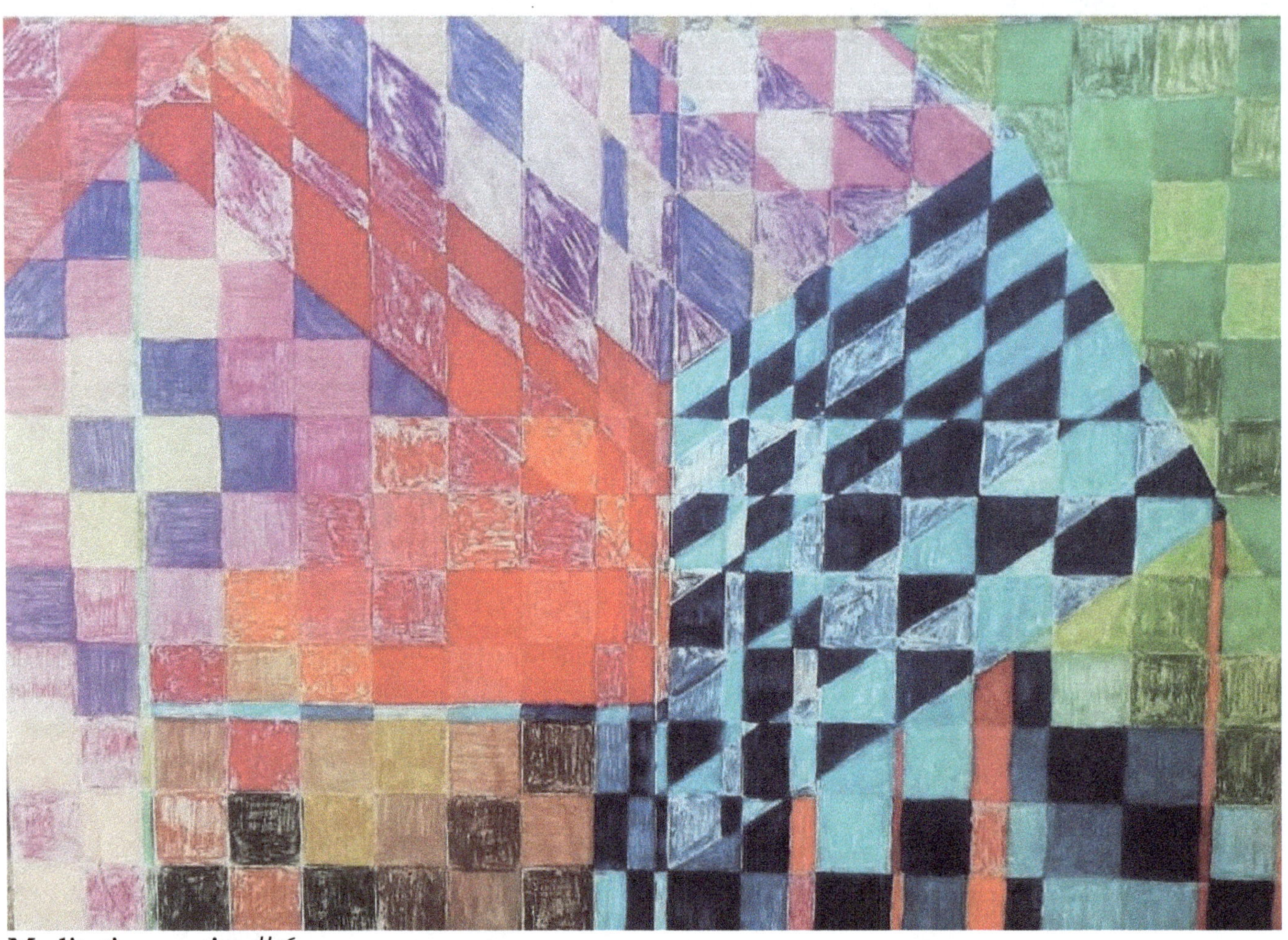

Meditations series # 6
Oil pastels, markets, felt pen and tip pen on white board
Size: 42cm by 59.4cm
Year: 2022

Consuming Light

As a young child and teen I gave Nyajezi River the gift of my soul, pouring dreams into its gently flowing light at the deep vastness of Dziva Rengwena, the horizontal long blanket lines of light of Tanganda falls, and the light cascading falls of paBirira. The colours of light moving were in Nyajezi's water and the wind. These colours of light moving were a pure language. As I grew older the language of the residual teen in me would throw skidding stones on the skins of the river's water, making patterns of flashing light. Until growing up removed boundaries, the confines of Nyajezi River were infinites the way the earth billions of years ago decided to spin around the all-giving sun without help, her slow movements endlessly repeating themselves. By the time I became an adult, the water and wind had darkened in the far away Hunyani River's stagnant pools of light. The river's dark light rising above the holding banks, burying the ghosts of the river banks' sparse trees. I could only hear the trickle of words in a language I think I understood but did not know, the way the city birds endlessly darts to and from wherever in the empty city skies with no trees to house the weightlessness of their songs. Grown up now means we are always going to the water and the mountain like a tree having diarrhea. Years later, in yonder boundaries, the ocean's waves folds onto the shore like a carpet unfolding into the floors, like a woman's contractual pushes, the way grief floods in unnoticed.

FYI. The fang of the woman metaphor, or you can say woman parable, is that woman is the force that moves the waves in the ocean. The skies are the gods that consumes the land. The land is the man that consumes the ocean, and the woman also consumes the land. The skies and oceans are always too consuming for man for the skies and oceans existed before man; they will exist after we are gone!

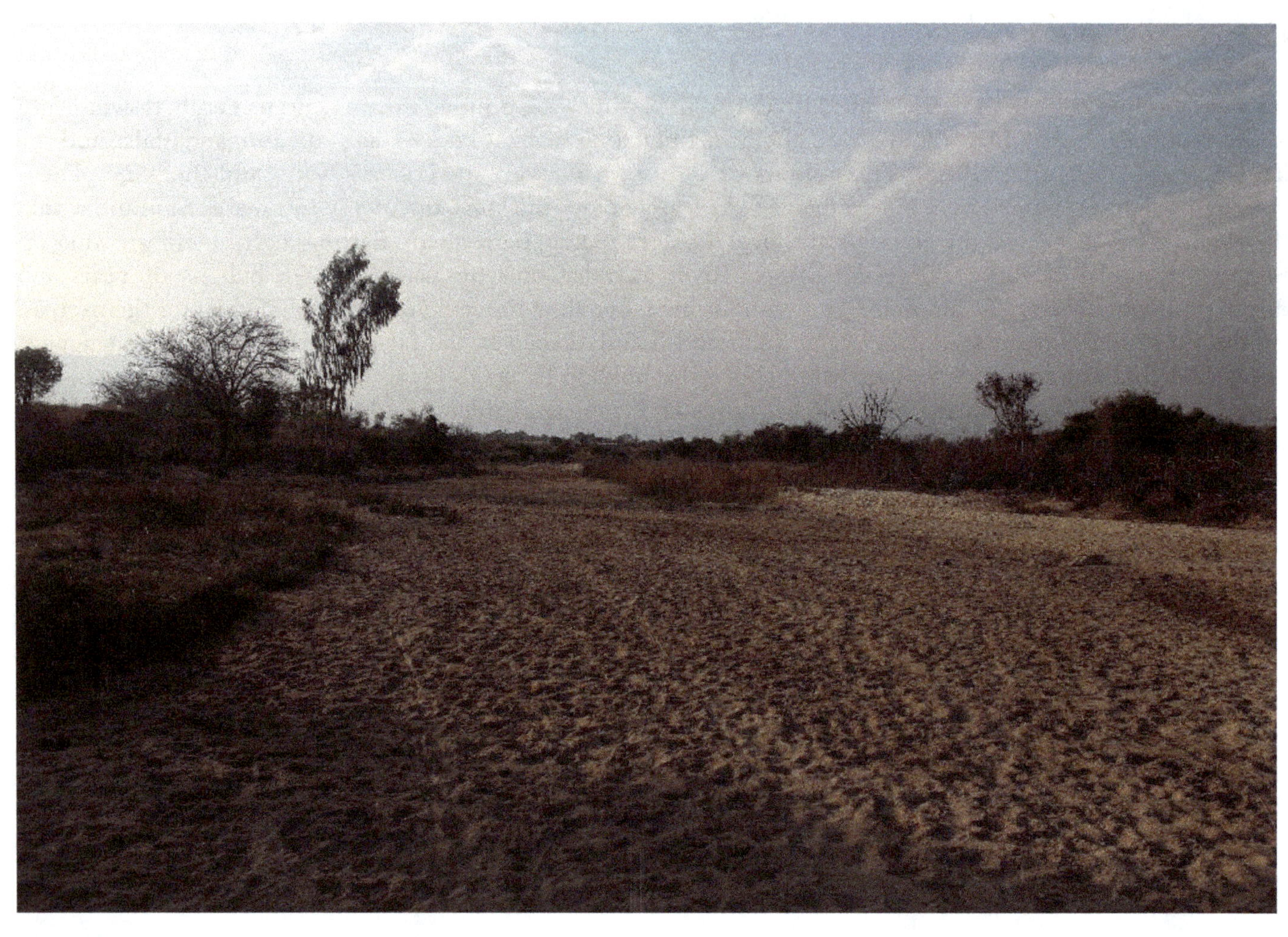

Nyajezi River,
Digital photography
September 2021, Nyanga, Zimbabwe

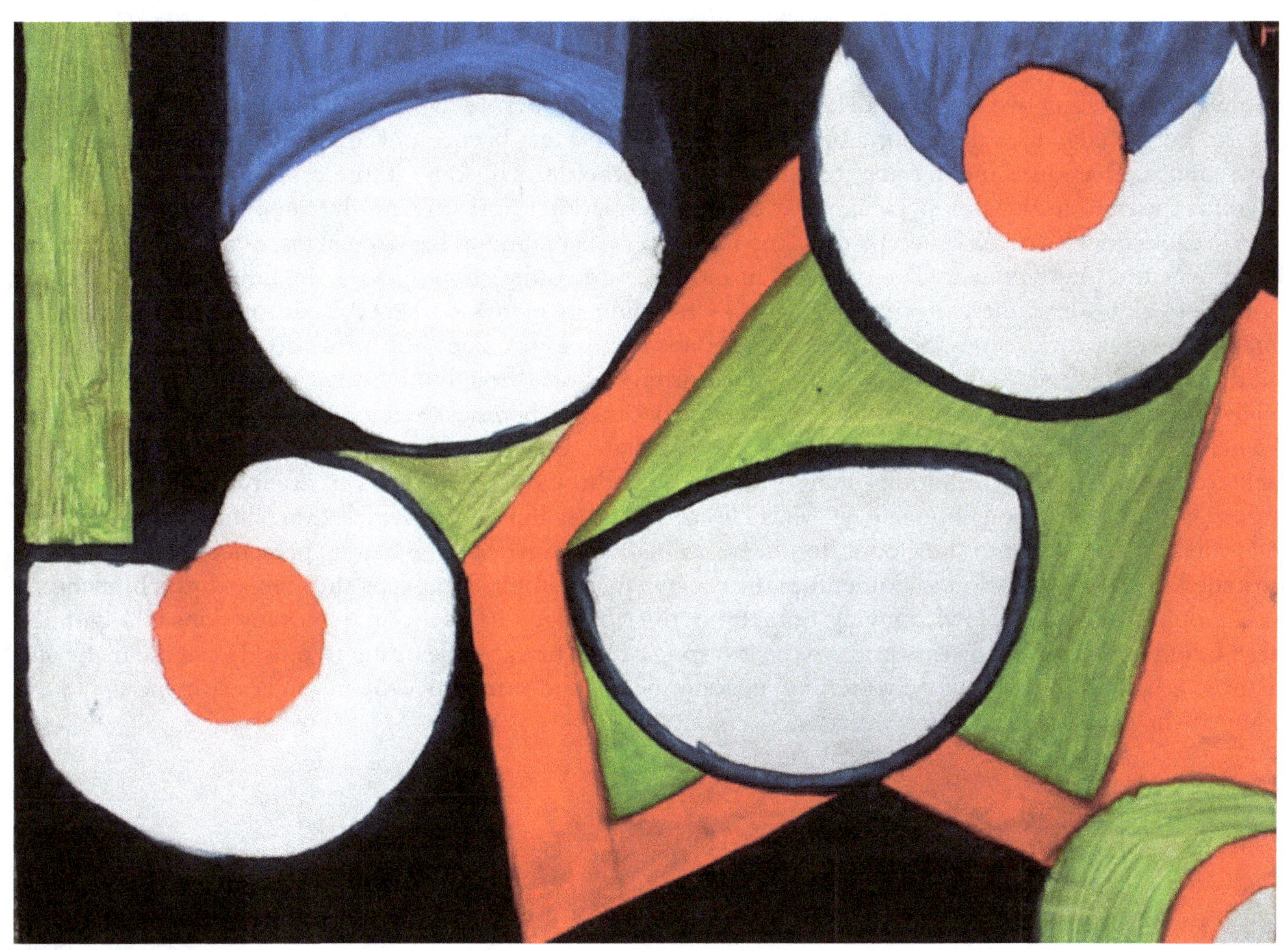

The white moons
Acrylics on canvass
Size: 45.7cm by 60.9cm
Year 2022

Sometimes the moon

The always competing two horizons delay themselves in a pause before night's fall, and the sun's lazy eye that had reached the edge eyes the moon's beguiling eye at this decline between evening and night, heralding the zen of things. Deep into the evening, the moon rests at the dermal skins of the eastern horizon; departed daylight is the thief to this moon, racing away unseen on the other horizon with the intent to snatch away this moon. Yellow prickles of blood seeps from the moon's eye as the moon's broken skins, as a brief warning of what moves the Owl's hunger. The moon is in motion, sometimes motionless, sometimes moored into an emotionless sky, sometimes lingering, sometimes escaping in night's darkened bedrooms, and sometimes forgetting its own dark secrets. Sometimes the moon is bright in the skies but forms no image on your mind. And the Blackbird's tail is fanned like a dark flame burning a hole through the canvassed sky as the blackbird's song is lost in a net of stars at the bottom of the sky's oceans. Sometimes the moon is like the lingering noises of witches on the prowl in shadowy nights of its faint light. One discord note sung by the Owl breaks the Blackbird's song. The Owl's hooting hungry eyes seeing through the shadows of a city gone to sleep; of vendors, of walls of walking humans, of ventricles of roads, of humus, of vehicles vanishing off. Sometimes the moon is a hunchback to the clouds, too heavy to be imprisoned, even when its presence continues to be threatened by the passing clouds. Sometimes the moon's pale complexion peeps through arthritic branches, a moon stripped of its legs, slowly moving. Sometimes the language of this moon tingles my skins into damned places I didn't know of, as my ears prick to the last song of the blackbird learning to quickly call the night out, like those creatures that reveals on your mind unannounced. And sometimes the moon is a soft sponge to the weight of the darkness we uncarry every day.

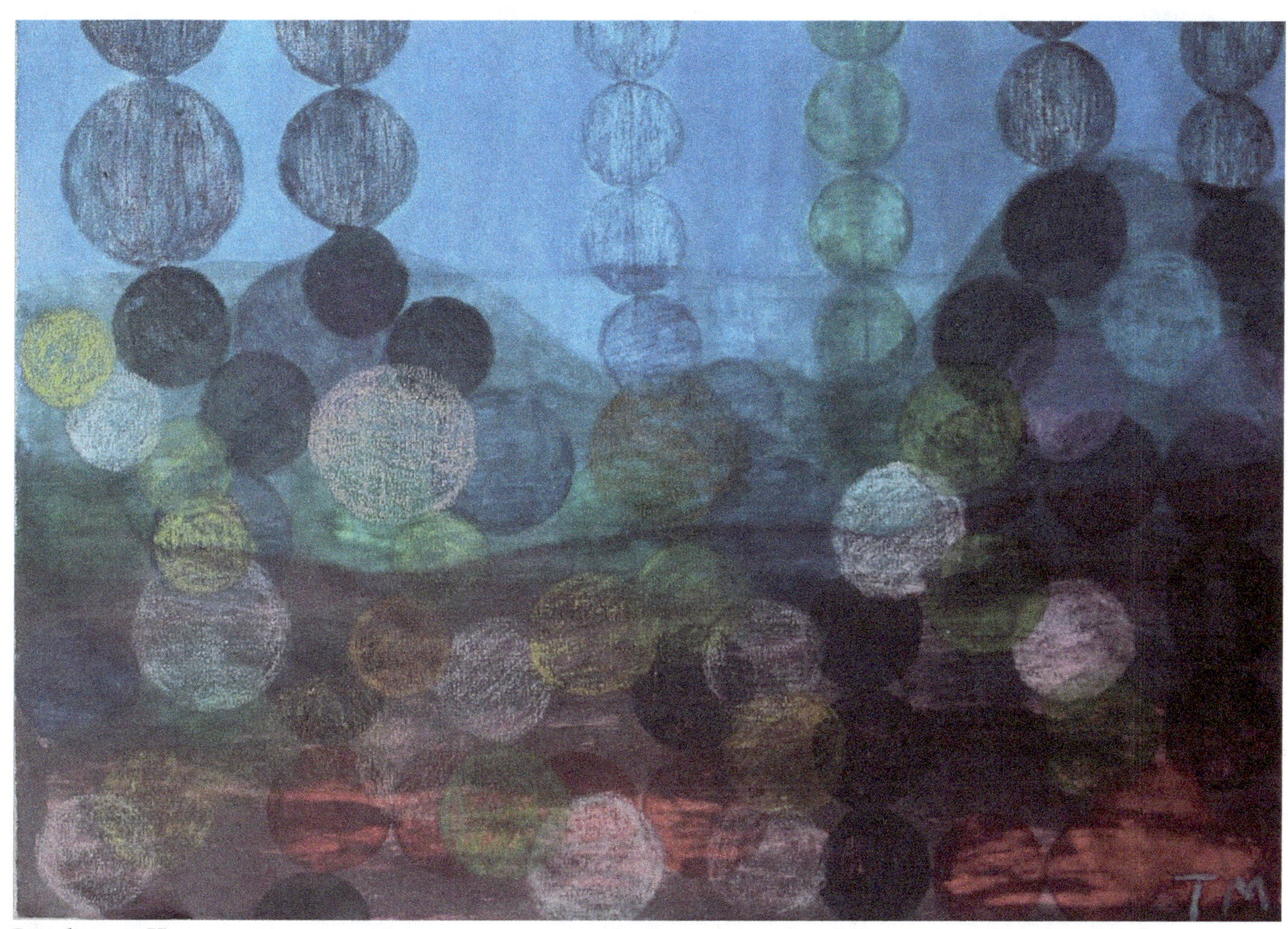

Landscape II
Watercolours, markers, oil pastels and acrylics on canvass
Size: 42cm by 59.4cm
2022

This is not the light of finding you

Outside, the sky's curtains open up to shower them with light filters of the sun' fires, coming from worlds beyond the sun they knew, taking its flames from that outer time they don't know; a time that has the limitation of time, a time that rearranges and dismantles earth's stagnant shadows and the mountain's rippling shadows. The sun they know imposes its will on broken walls for homes and still cold forgotten rooms, and if the bricks of these broken walls were tears, the sun's light desalinates them. The bricks now lend into the rooms several chords of light. The rooms' curtains are still a board to limit the amount of light intruding from the outside. The rooms have enough light that's not going anywhere like a candle's flames spreading undefined shadows across the room… an ambiguousness of fragmented shapes appearing and disappearing at the axis of the confusion between the colours. These colours are always nothing without light!

He writes in weeping light, his pen bleeding his heart on the page, baptizing his day with emptiness that is only filled up by this ritual of writing. Writing presences, absences, immanence, exigencies, impermanence, as poems that writes permanence on the lines of light that collects in the greys of his head like leftover dreams. The shape of his voice is the shape of wings; he moves his writer's voice onto the light to see what would maim him. Bit by bit he is prey to light, caught in the cycle of watching the sun's gradual disintegration, as the darkness dissipate around him.

The weight of light he carries every day from this thread of sunlight challenges his presence, leaves a reflection on both their eyes and light as if from air. The dead in her light absorbs light from his eyes, a dull light now intrudes on the brightness behind her eyes. She has absorbed all his personal memories while crossing through them. He now resides behind the shadows of giving up, stolen imaginations and memories waning away into darkness. The darkness that seek the lowlands with a wish of a changing light, trying and failing so hard to inhabit the light, seeing only with the sound of Turner's broken brushes, brushing the skies in drunken strokes

Counting the moments, one by one, wondering if a part of him has grown unnoticed by him, whilst also accounting for the silent corners where this poem whispers to an attentive mind. But for now he can only attract light.

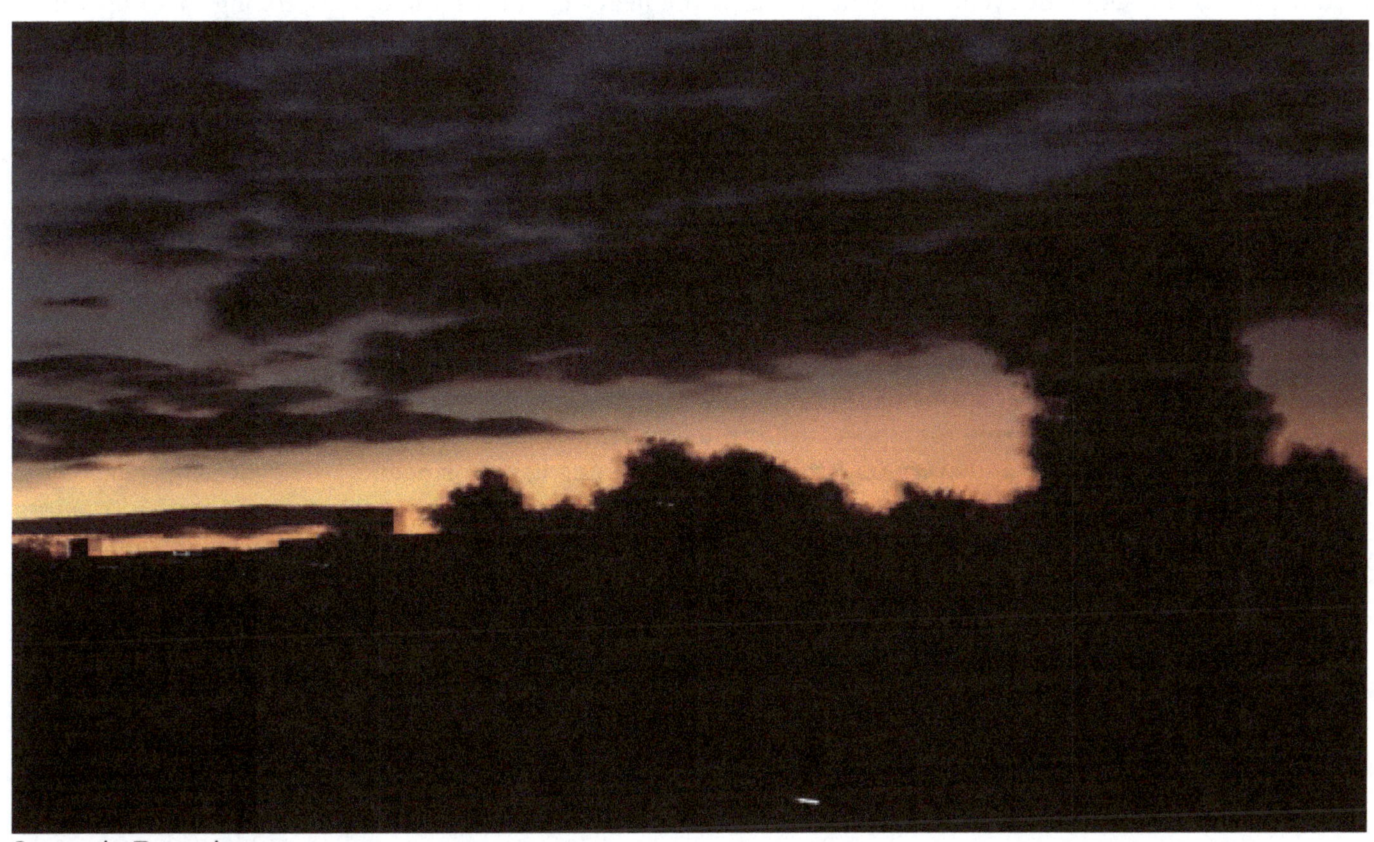

Sunset in Pretoria,
Digital photography
March 2022, Pretoria, South Africa

Repainting the landscapes of Cyclone Ida

Silence creeps through an open sky like something continuous. The wind pecks at the tree leaves as they move to the melody of a hymn of birds fluttering in the trees that have forgotten the value of silence. Understanding the secrets of changing skies, the erosions of the wind, as the doors and windows rattle an unfamiliar tune of held breath of a cyclone delayed. The wind unwarps the heavy clouds of the clouds, roiling them up with a mean interpretation. Autumnal branches whipped up by the angry skies. A robin drinks from the clouds, each seep rippling down. The wind plays another tune and another and another…

Early darkness claiming its territory of dark, educated in a science that ascends beyond understanding the darkening of time. The falling skies closing their doors on the air we breathe as the sharp teeth of the storm eyed and devoured Chimanimani. In safe places, every night we watch them as they fall away into the floods, hundreds of their voices in our heads, screaming with pain even though their lips were unmoving. Their insane thrusts to live into the panic of the betraying skies, as the storm's hostility submit to no man's prayers. My mind vomits at the possibility of counting into infinity as they drift away.

The farmers still searching for a rope or strand to follow home, and those in strong homes huddling together in corners of rooms as if posing for a postcard to the heavens, listening to the sounds of cold sea gods. The storms have swallowed each and every fragment of the remaining light, tormenting the light of its nakedness, kicking it out. A night betrayed by its assurances, by the storm's spilling moods, seducing the shadows into homes. A single Mubvee tree sways as though in gentle breeze and with the rush of anger the wind throws Mubvee's sausage fruits to the ground.

When this creature has fed and now hides from its killing moments, the forest will have its own perpetual processes of illness, symptoms, bedridden days, dying, recovery, stitching together the tapestry of living, and time will repaint this landscape on the minds that will ponder about this beautiful place.

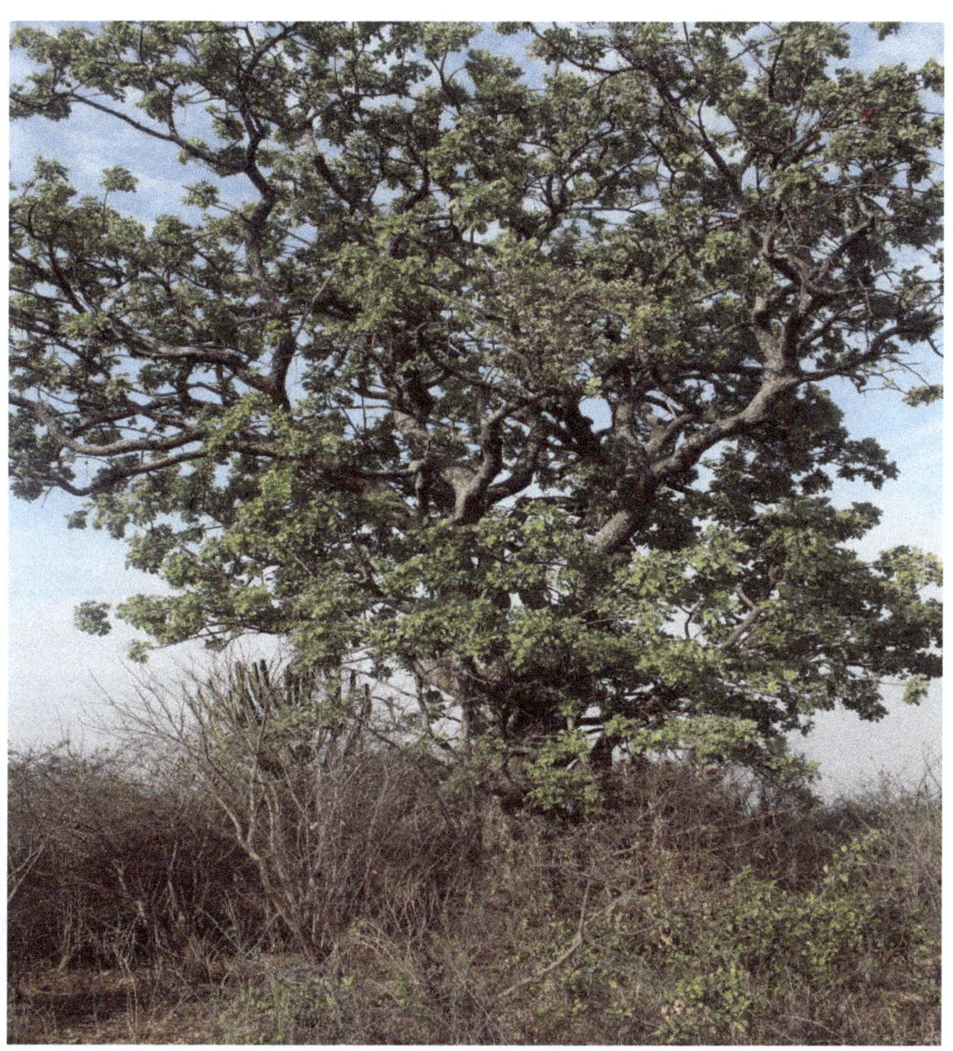

Mubvee Tree (Sausage Tree)
Digital photography
September 2021, Nyanga, Zimbabwe

We built this city of poetry

To the poets out there sing with me this Starship song, *We Built This City*, of poetry. The beauty of discovering new *old* music is that you create your own memories independent of others. When you discover me here you are discovering me alone without imperial syntax. No hail to the peer-reviewed goitered rivers for this African poet. Know that Africans are always the baby thrown out with the water by the world that doesn't want us and walking is the same as running, walk but especially run- sitting hurts you. For perfect body is no body. The journey is time neither silent nor sleeping

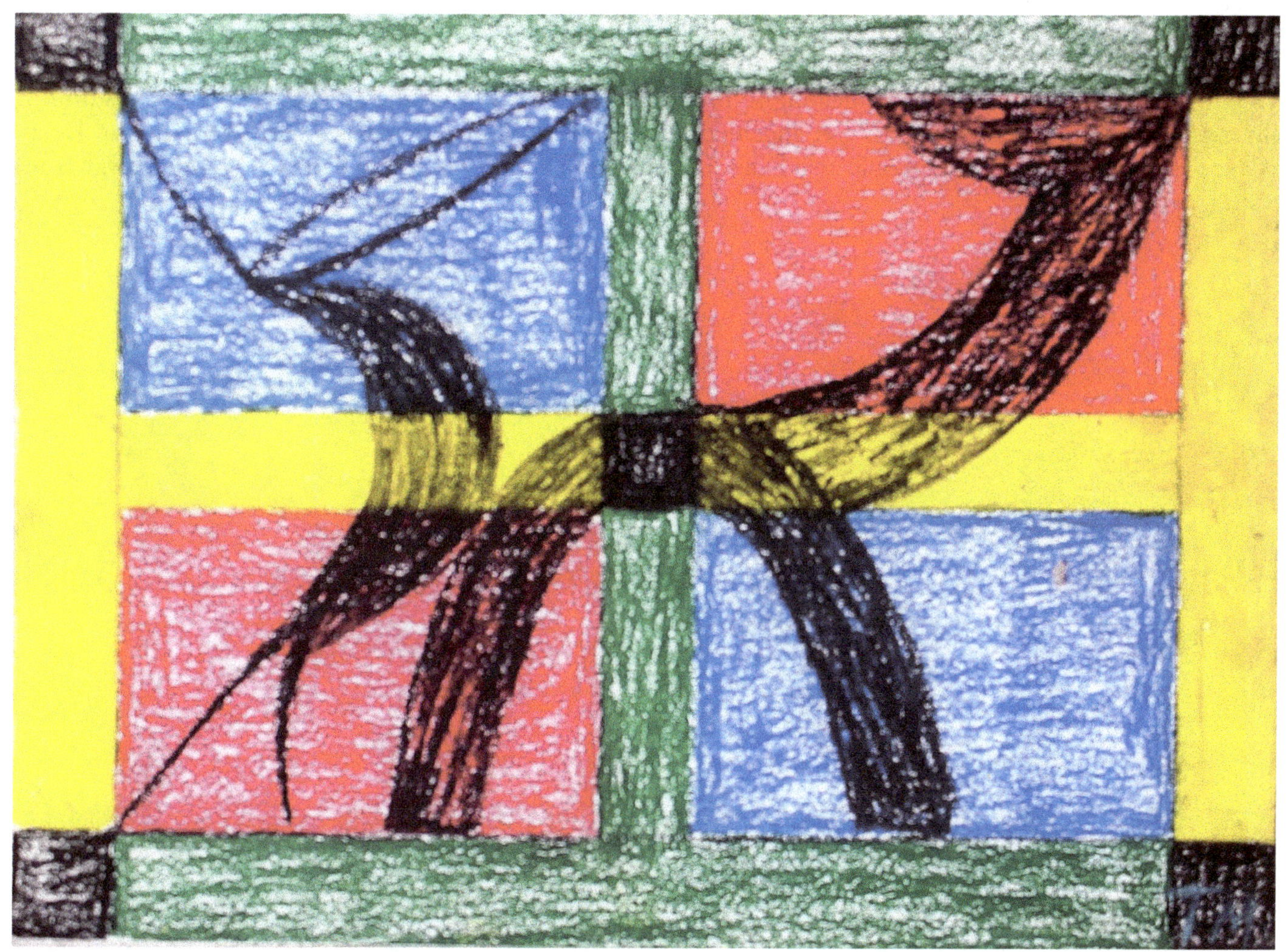

Let's dance II
Oil pastels on fabriano paper
29.7cm by 42cm
Year: 2022

Every bad thing is a new frontier

Trying to reason with eight is like medicating to the ghosts whilst knowing the eerie truth that ghosts do not really exists like the tender mercies of a chance encounter with a mind as sharp as a narrow argument. Every bad thing is a new frontier, and I would also like to mention the blind, wandering 8 octave pointing away from the straight…

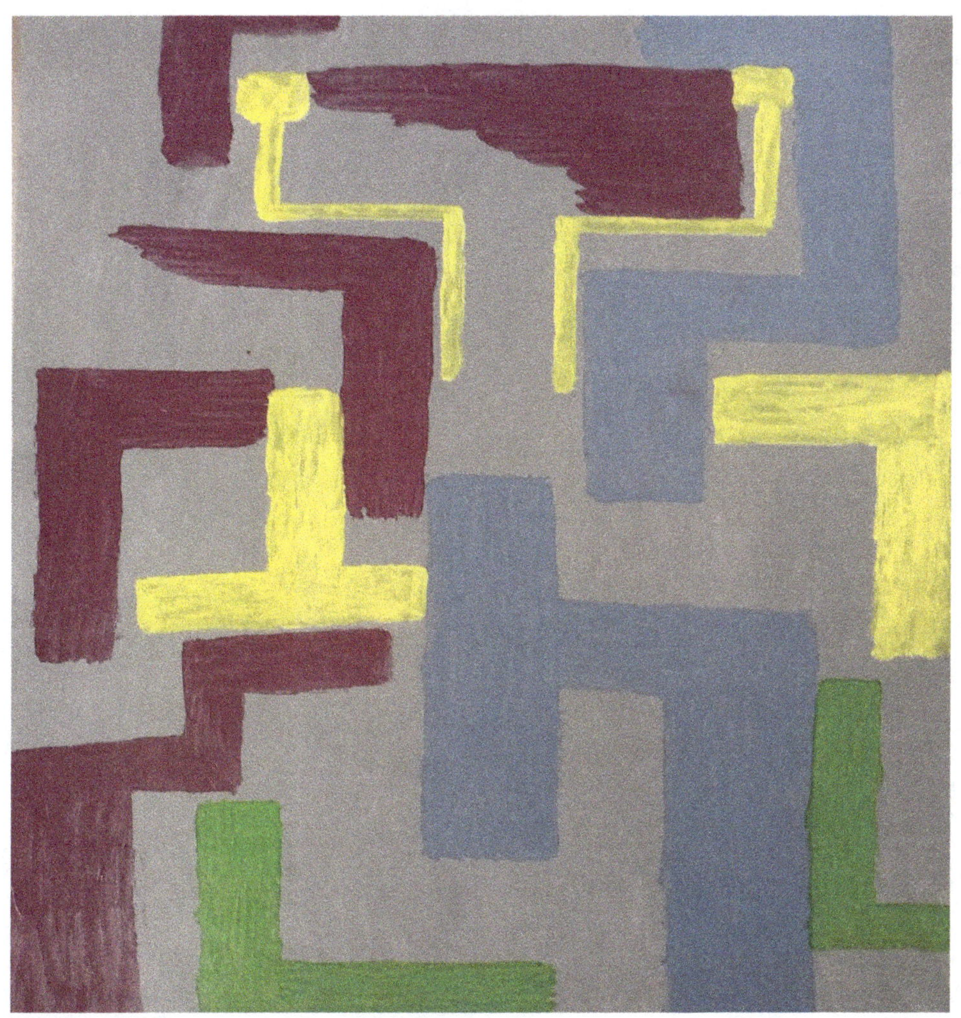

Humanoid human
Acrylics on paper
Size: 42cm by 59.4cm
2023

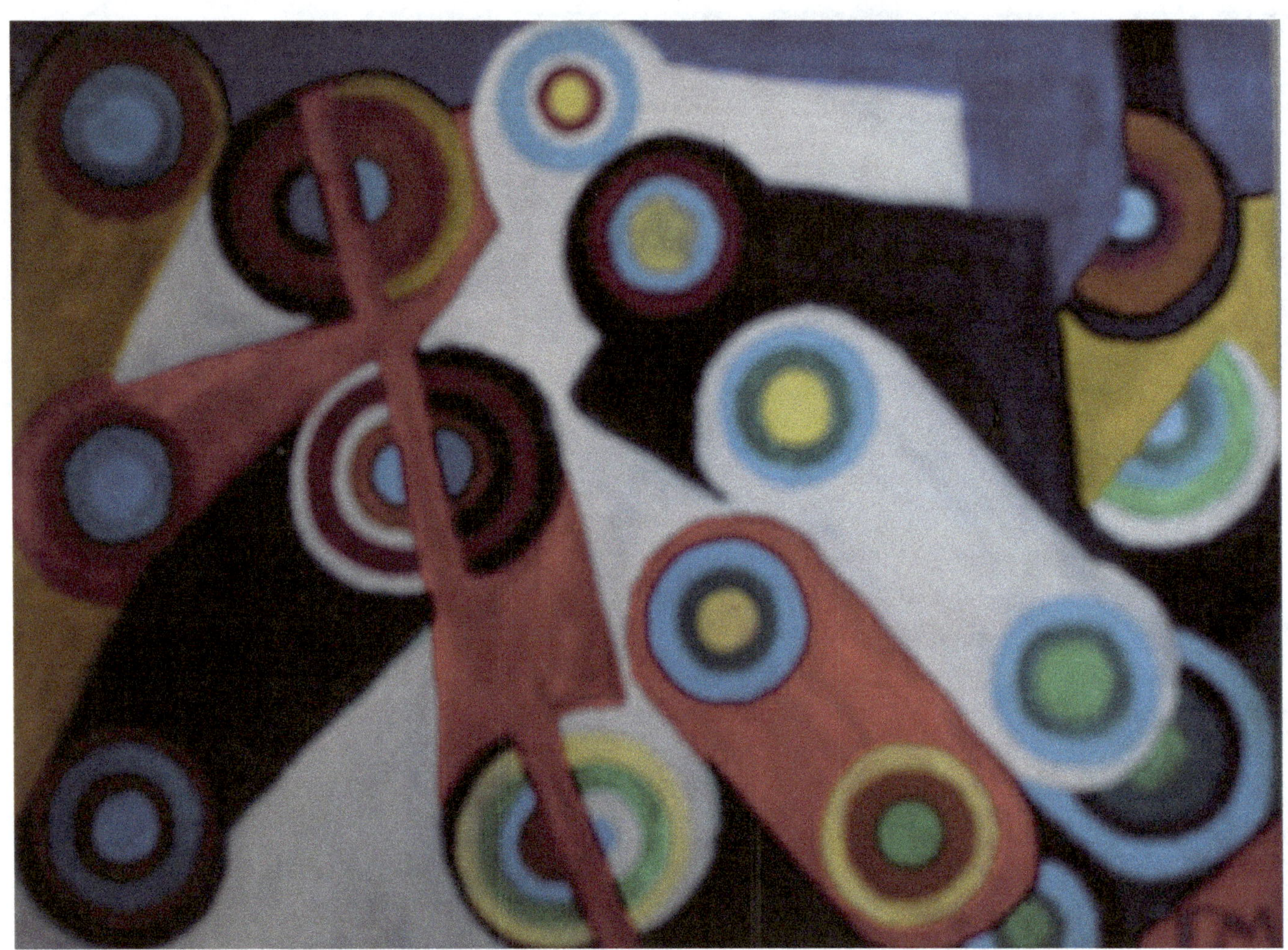

Meditation series #2
Acrylics on canvass
Size: 42cm by 59.4cm
Year: 2022

Meditation series #2

This painting harnesses engineering – how parts are interlinked and interconnected in such as a way to propel each toward movement. It's like how the lower parts of a locomotive train are joined in circles, blocks, circular, half circular parts that helps to propel a train to move- faster. This is the concept I harness. All circular things are endowed with the power to move, eg the earth, the planets, and like a fool I will include the moon and sun, the balls in a game of soccer, tennis etc, the wheels of a bus goes round and round, the train, bicycle etc… These are the circles of thought, each is imbued with the power to move, to change, to infuse newness thereby creating a graph of a moving mind. I am a colour and line composer, the colours drives composition in all sorts of ways; the blues, the greens, the whites, the greys… deepen, the creams, maroons, browns etc… propels the thoughts.

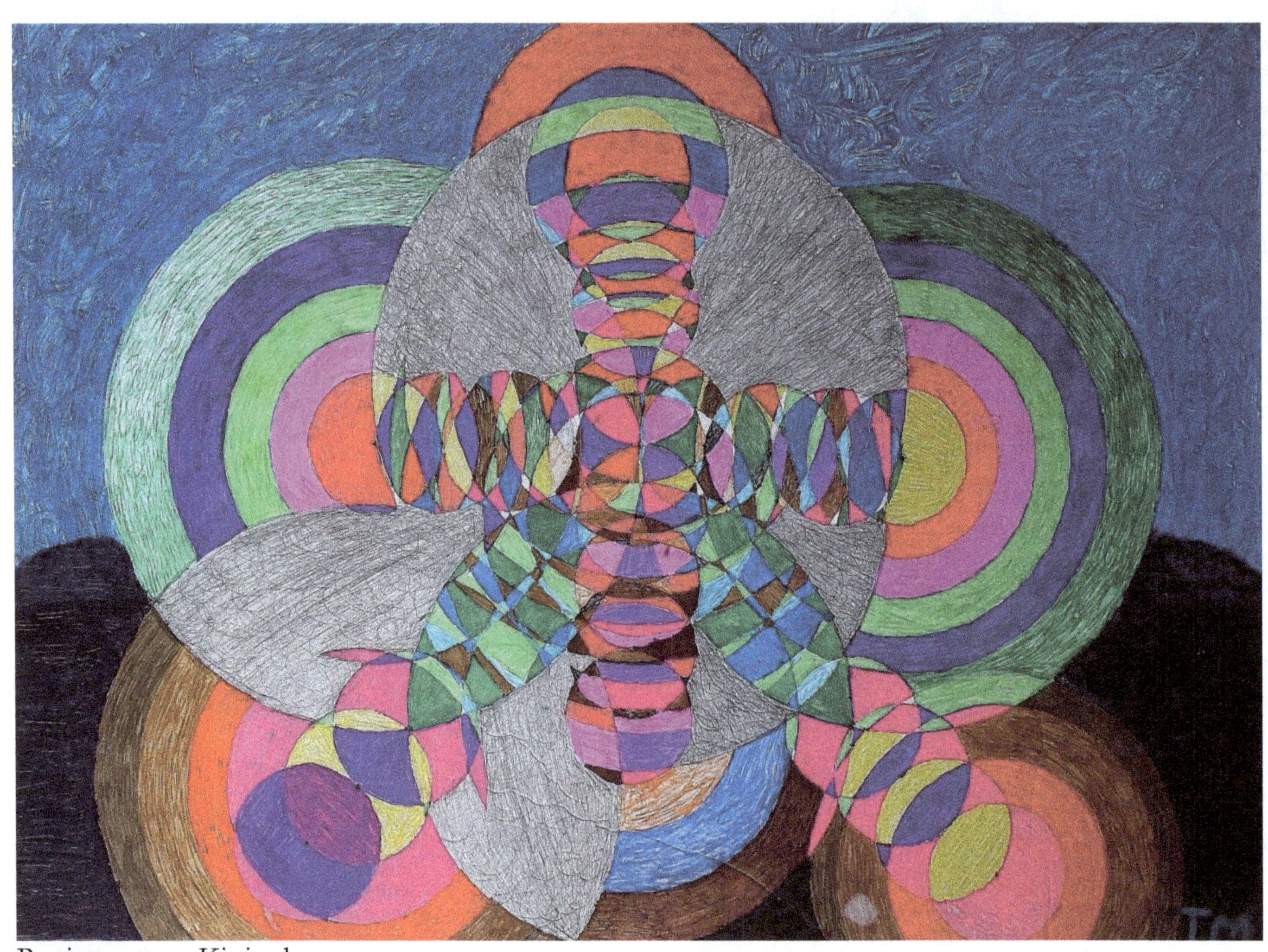

Persian pattern Kittiwake
Felt pens, tip pens, acrylics and graphite on white board
Size: 42cm by 59.4cm
2022

When you have chanted 10 times

You sit together as if waiting for the right time to dream, sitting together nearly touching, this is your opening. Actions take hold of your hands like testimony to hungry minds. Your interiors are ten years unchanged, younger as the ripples of the muscles of your hearts; they show no signpost of recent decay as if time had locked where there is no key. Your lips press together guiding your thoughts in a rare moment of passion. Your hungers are the shape of triangles. You peel her skirt and launch your thoughts through her wet prayer, feeling her housing you, sucking your beating heart stick…

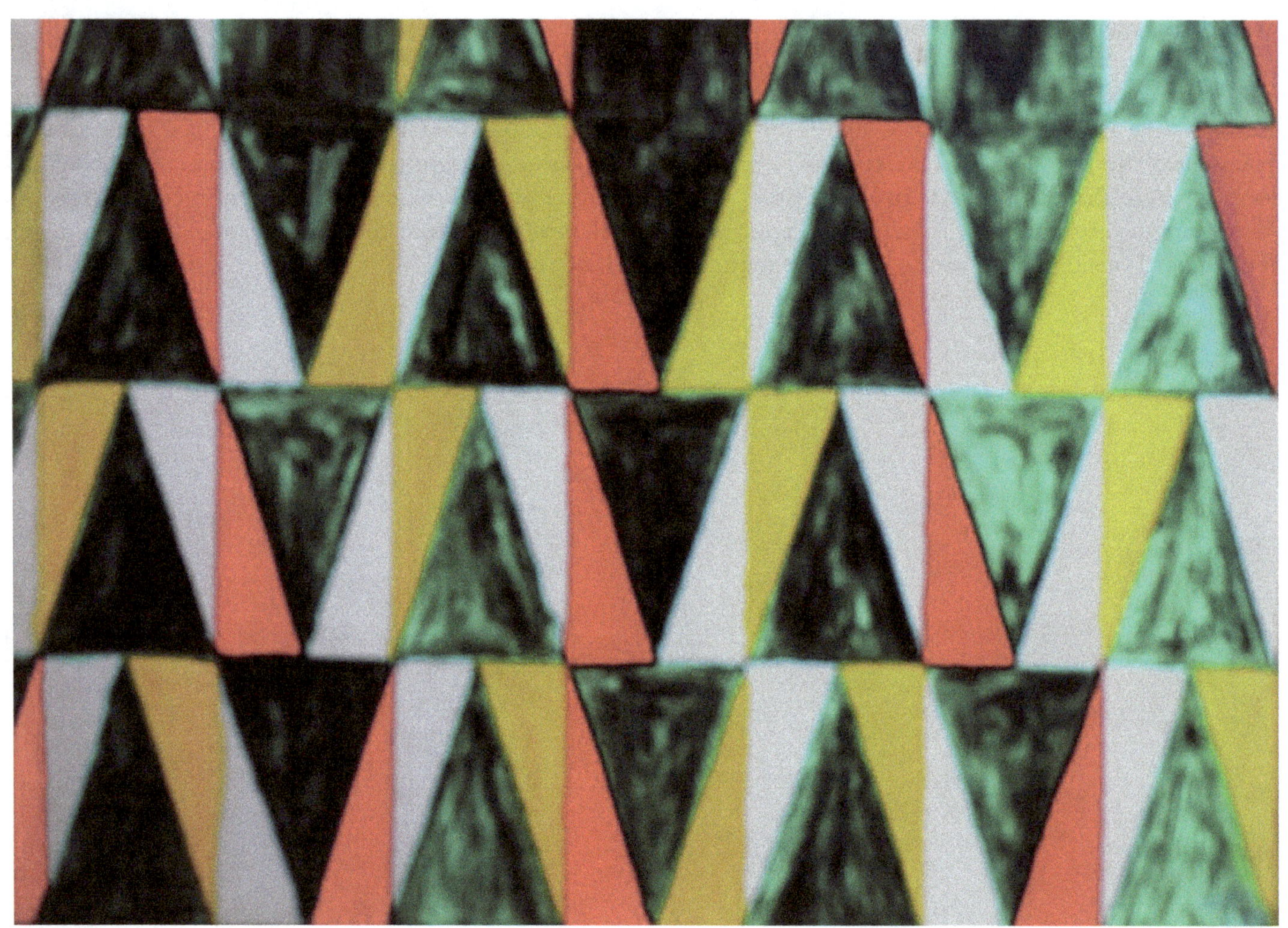

Meditations series # 7
Acrylics on white board
Size: 42cm by 59.4cm
Year: 2022

Meditations series # 7

Triangulars of greens, whites, reds create horizontal music. I started with the green colour…the green colour is the music of hope. The red colour is the music of passion, the yellow colour is the music of newness and freshness as of yellow roses, and the white colour is the music of purity. This is another architectural painting that uses planes, lines and colours to create linearity and music. I am continuing that wrestling away with colours as language which I did with the painting *Meditation series #3*

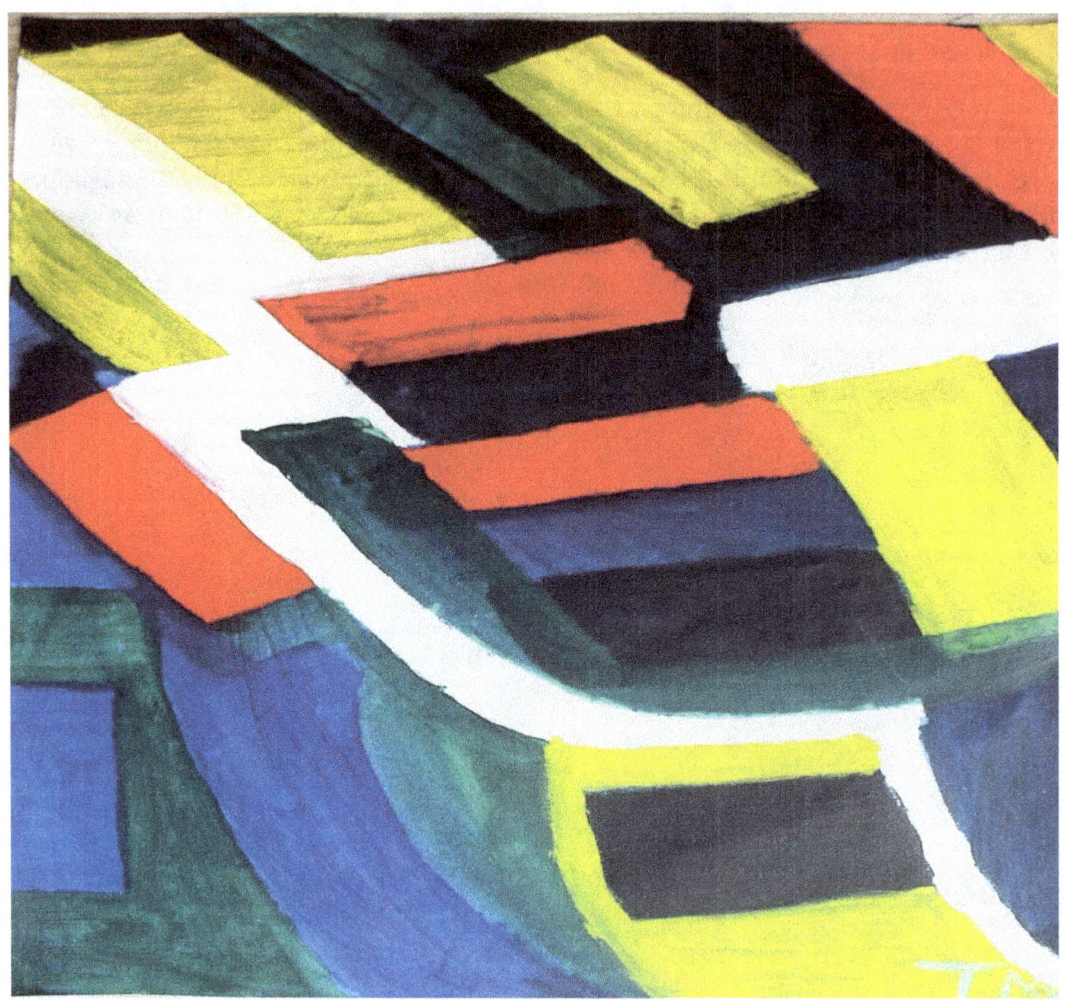

Meditations series # 8
Acrylics on canvass
Size: 42cm by 59.4cm
Year: 2022

For her, the Lake and him

Arriving for the second time at the lake, she slips into its meanings. Floating leaves are floating boats on the lake's imaginations taking the depth of thought beyond the end winds. Fish jumping out of the water are stretching the question marks before diving back into the water. Falling through coloured dreams, like an exclamation mark, stones she throws into the lake shoot down to the bottom of it. Everything she touches is stolen by a shadow of years, striding past its irreversible pasts. Her life is boxes full of empty todays. For her the place known as past is a source of pain and profit, she paid for this poem for you. A poem unpolishing the words he could never share, testing her memories- a poem the universe of empty pages.

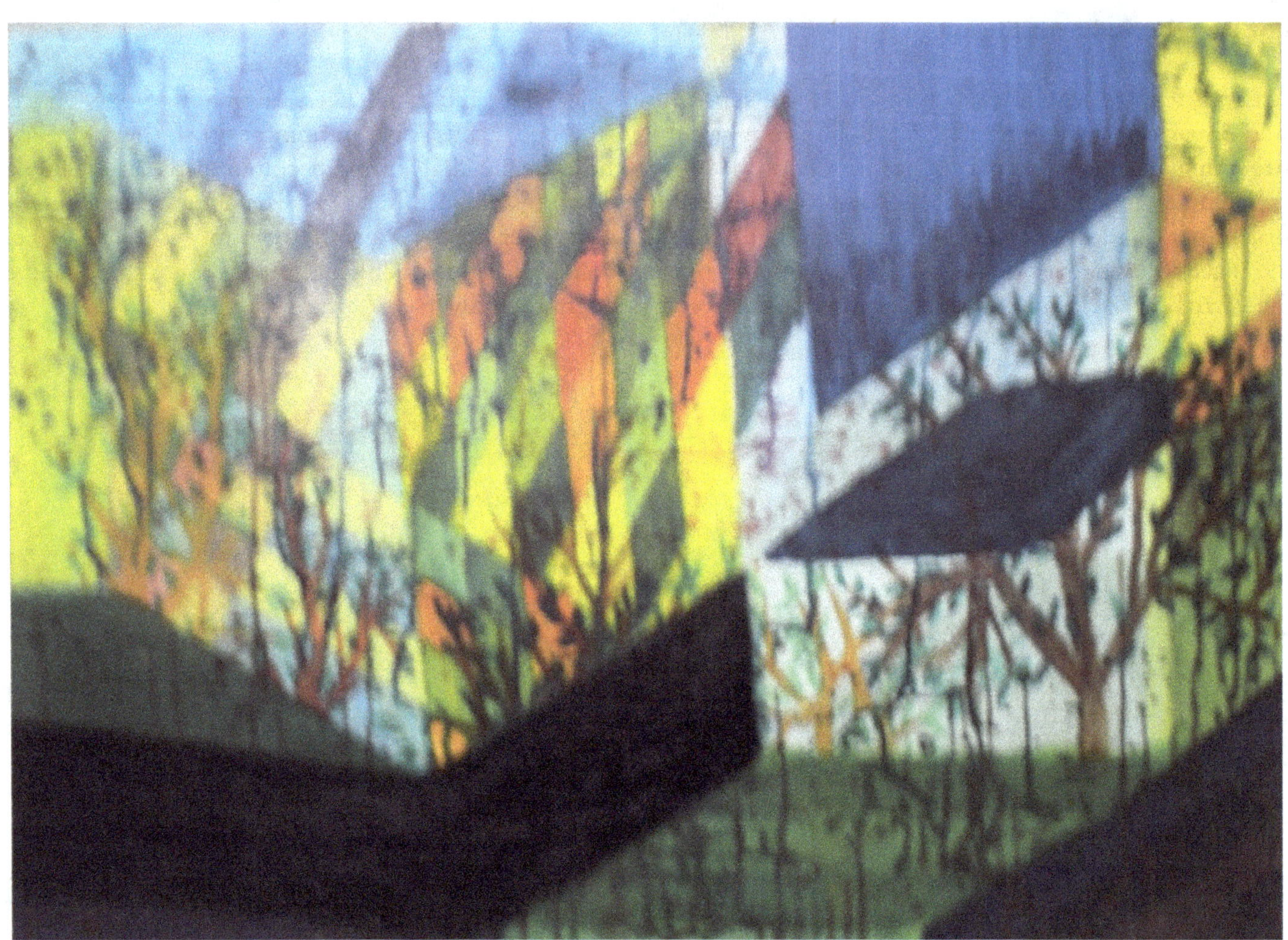

Post Covid 19 hallucinations
Size: 59.4cm by 80.1cm
Acrylics on canvass
Year: 2022

Post Covid 19 hallucinations

Covid 19 hallucinations still attack us every day as the thoughts of the last three years remind us of how as a human race we faced the brink and lost so much of who we were. There is still that architectural play with the city structures, roads, buildings, trees, and the ever-persistent covid 19 viruses that seemed to cover the whole landscape in lines, splotches, dots of paints. Making the outsides of this city unlivable. There is that time when the whole world stayed indoors and with the painting I was proposing the question, what if this was going to be our new normal

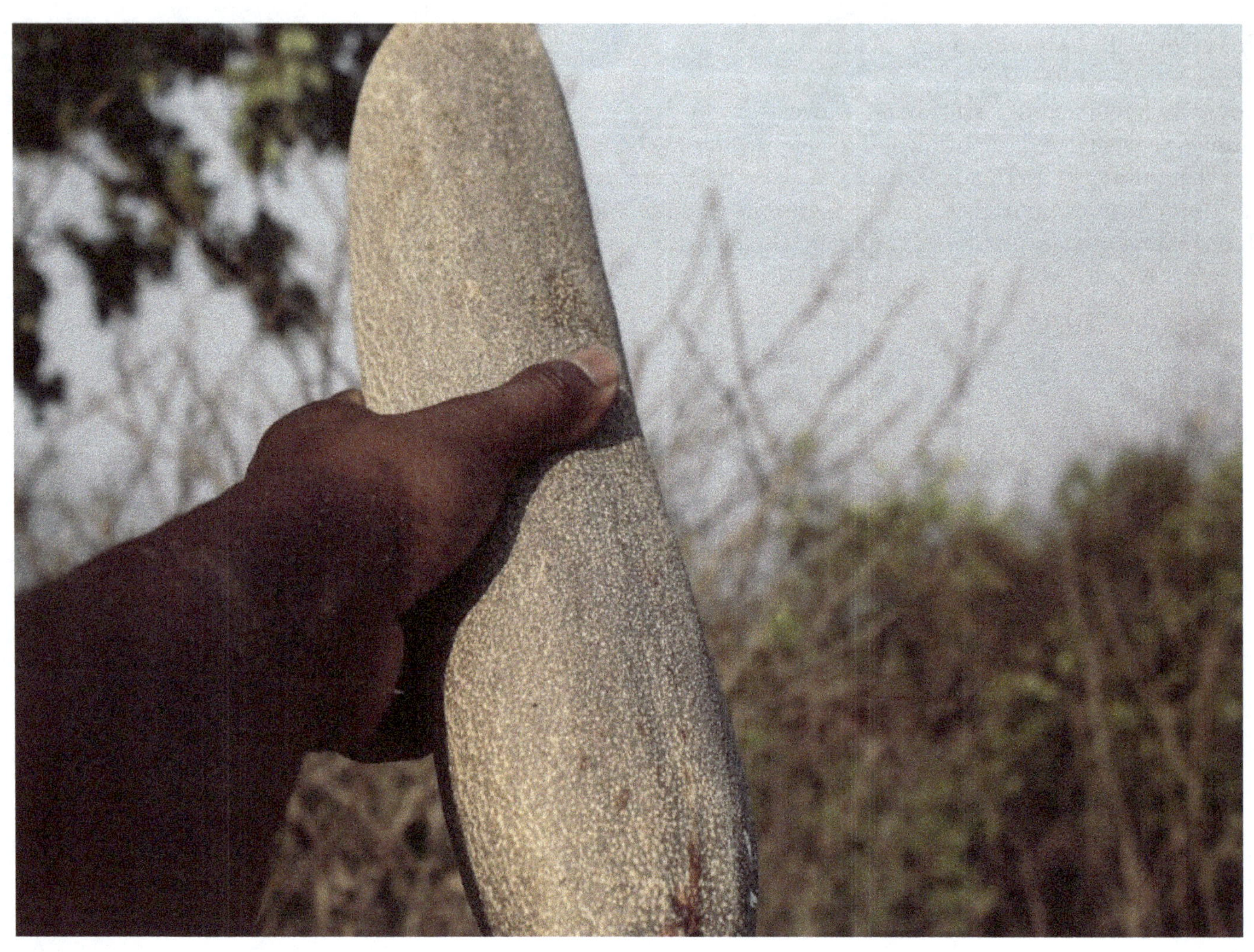

Sausage fruit,
Digital photography
September 2021, Nyanga, Zimbabwe

The crows in my poetry

The tragedy of limbless form is it affirms life and death. A conversation of grief loaned to those who never speak, acknowledging their mourning with a shake of heads, embracing grief with a practiced frown.

In another home a child wonders why her father sleeps in a white clothed box whilst silly men and women try to talk to a sleeping man, deceiving their senses into believing autumn will never end.

In the fields a halo of crows signposts the place where a man will lie

And then the crows ride on the shaft of air's back into silence as they eat the skies to the west, leaving their song huffs inside empty pieces of the skies.

It's only these black doves' haunts that witnesses his silenced body's shut eyes as he creeps into the landscape in seamless whites. Us breathing the pain of a grief only he can hear.

In a home, a few villages over, a crow pounces at chicken's chicks, leaving a blood abstract of their deaths.

These crows in my poetry are always ready to peck at every metaphor whilst trying to listen to the green noises of summer.

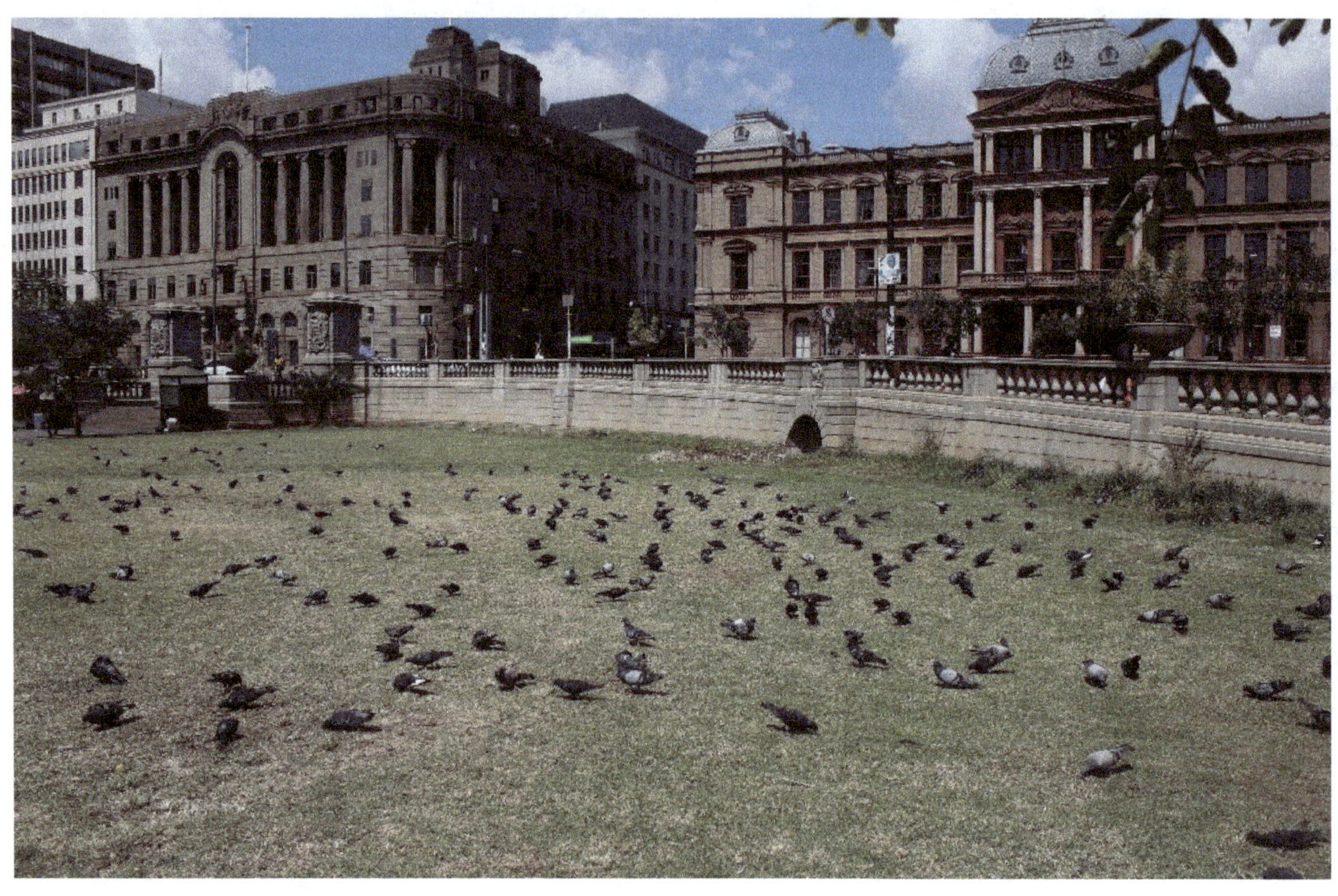

Pigeons of Pretoria,
Digital photography
March 2022, Pretoria, South Africa

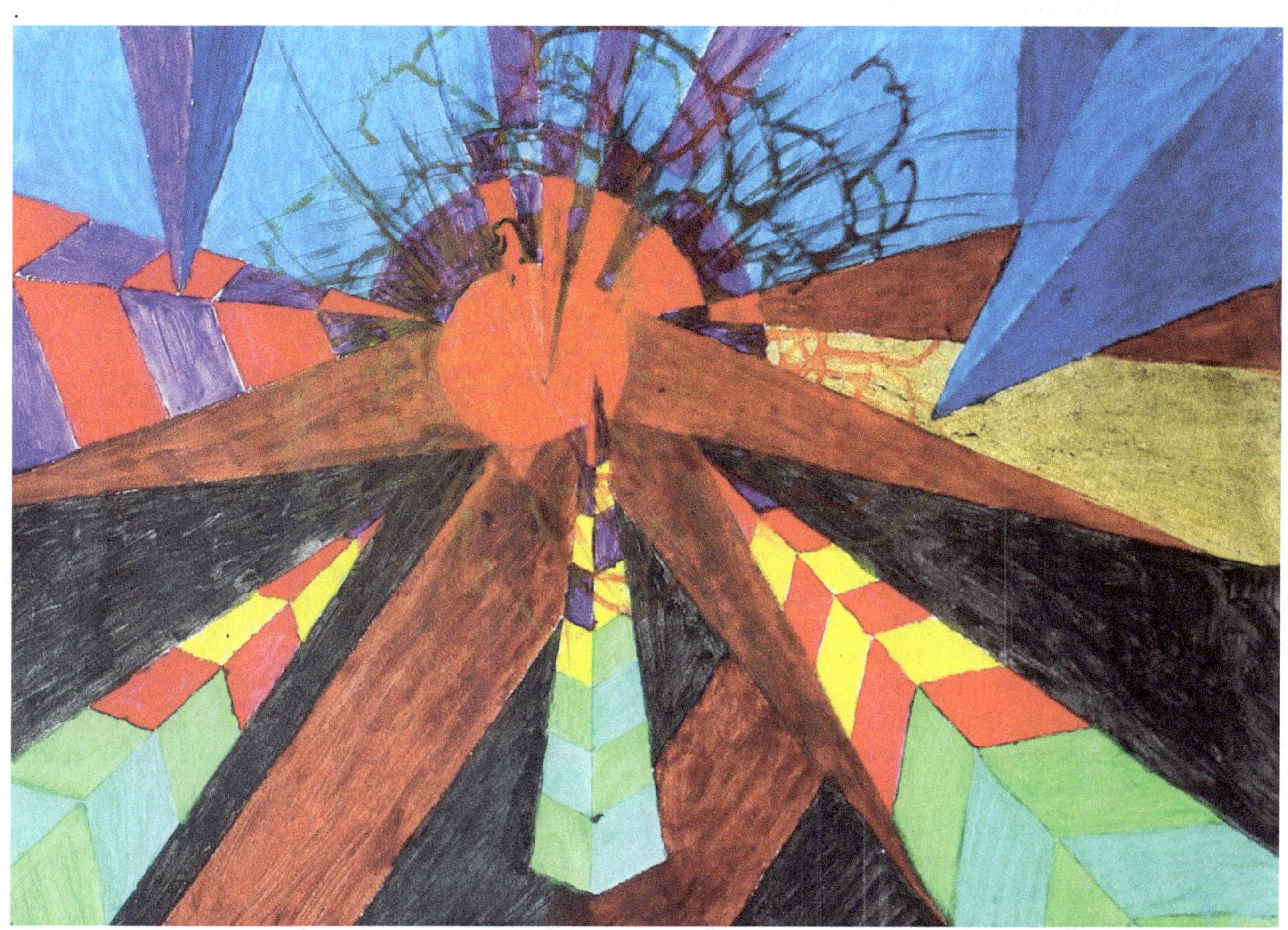

The Setting Sun
Watercolours, acrylics on fabriano paper
Size: 42cm by 59.4cm
2022

Mmap New African Poets Series

If you have enjoyed *Of poets, gods, ghosts. Irritants and storytellers*, consider these other fine books in the **Mmap New African Poets Series** from *Mwanaka Media and Publishing*:

I Threw a Star in a Wine Glass by Fethi Sassi
Best New African Poets 2017 Anthology by Tendai R Mwanaka and Daniel Da Purificacao
Logbook Written by a Drifter by Tendai Rinos Mwanaka
Mad Bob Republic: Bloodlines, Bile and a Crying Child by Tendai Rinos Mwanaka
Zimbolicious Poetry Vol 1 by Tendai R Mwanaka and Edward Dzonze
Zimbolicious Poetry Vol 2 by Tendai R Mwanaka and Edward Dzonze
Zimbolicious: An Anthology of Zimbabwean Literature and Arts, Vol 3 by Tendai Mwanaka
Under The Steel Yoke by Jabulani Mzinyathi
Fly in a Beehive by Thato Tshukudu
Bounding for Light by Richard Mbuthia
Sentiments by Jackson Matimba
Best New African Poets 2018 Anthology by Tendai R Mwanaka and Nsah Mala
Words That Matter by Gerry Sikazwe
The Ungendered by Delia Watterson
Ghetto Symphony by Mandla Mavolwane
Sky for a Foreign Bird by Fethi Sassi
A Portrait of Defiance by Tendai Rinos Mwanaka
Zimbolicious: An Anthology of Zimbabwean Literature and Arts, Vol 4 by Tendai Mwanaka and Jabulani Mzinyathi
When Escape Becomes the only Lover by Tendai R Mwanaka
ويَسهَرُ اللَّيلُ عَلَى شَفَتي...وَالغَمَام by Fethi Sassi
A Letter to the President by Mbizo Chirasha
This is not a poem by Richard Inya
Pressed flowers by John Eppel
Righteous Indignation by Jabulani Mzinyathi:
Blooming Cactus by Mikateko Mbambo
Rhythm of Life by Olivia Ngozi Osouha

Travellers Gather Dust and Lust by Gabriel Awuah Mainoo
Chitungwiza Mushamukuru: An Anthology from Zimbabwe's Biggest Ghetto Town by Tendai Rinos Mwanaka
Zimbolicious: An Anthology of Zimbabwean Literature and Arts, Vol 5 by Tendai Mwanaka
Because Sadness is Beautiful? by Tanaka Chidora
Of Fresh Bloom and Smoke by Abigail George
Shades of Black by Edward Dzonze
Best New African Poets 2020 Anthology by Tendai Rinos Mwanaka, Lorna Telma Zita and Balddine Moussa
This Body is an Empty Vessel by Beaton Galafa
Between Places by Tendai Rinos Mwanaka
Best New African Poets 2021 Anthology by Tendai Rinos Mwanaka, Lorna Telma Zita and Balddine Moussa
Zimbolicious: An Anthology of Zimbabwean Literature and Arts, Vol 6 by Tendai Mwanaka and Chenjerai Mhondera
A Matter of Inclusion by Chad Norman
Keeping the Sun Secret by Mariel Awendit
سِجلٌّ مَكتُوبٌ لثَائِهٍ by Tendai Rinos Mwanaka
Ghetto Blues by Tendai Rinos Mwanaka
Zimbolicious: An Anthology of Zimbabwean Literature and Arts, Vol 7 by Tendai Rinos Mwanaka and Tanaka Chidora
Best New African Poets 2022 Anthology by Tendai Rinos Mwanaka and Helder Simbad
Dark Lines of History by Sithembele Isaac Xhegwana
a sky is falling by Nica Cornell
Death of a Statue by Samuel Chuma
Along the way by Jabulani Mzinyathi
Strides of Hope by Tawanda Chigavazira
Young Galaxies by Abigail George
Coming of Age by Gift Sakirai
Mother's Kitchen and Other Places by Antreka. M. Tladi
Best New African Poets 2023 Anthology by Tendai Rinos Mwanaka, Helder Simbad and Gerald Mpesse
Zimbolicious Anthology Vol 8 by Tendai Rinos Mwanaka and Mathew T Chikono

Soon to be released
Formless by Raïs Neza Boneza

Broken Maps by Riak Marial Riak

https://facebook.com/MwanakaMediaAndPublishing/